Media Track List

Audio and video can be found in the *Inside Listening and Speaking* Digital Download Center. Go to www.insidelisteningandspeaking.com. Click on the Video Center 🔲 for streaming video. Click on the Audio Center 🔊 and choose to stream or download ⬇ the audio file you select.

UNIT 1

Listening	Listen	🔊	ILS_L2_U1_Listen1
	Listen for Main Ideas	🔊	ILS_L2_U1_Listen1
	Apply B	🔊	ILS_L2_U1_Listen_ApplyB
	Apply C	🔊	ILS_L2_U1_Listen_ApplyC
Speaking	Listen	🔊	ILS_L2_U1_Listen2
	Listen for Main Ideas	🔊	ILS_L2_U1_Listen2
	Apply C	🔊	ILS_L2_U1_Listen2
Pronunciation	Learn A	🔊	ILS_L2_U1_Pron_LearnA
	Learn B	🔊	ILS_L2_U1_Pron_LearnB
	Apply A	🔊	ILS_L2_U1_Pron_ApplyA
End of Unit Task	B	🔊	ILS_L2_U1_End_B
	C	🔊	ILS_L2_U1_End_C

UNIT 2

Listening	Watch	🔲	ILS_L2_U2_Watch1
	Listen for Main Ideas	🔲	ILS_L2_U2_Watch1
	Apply B	🔲	ILS_L2_U2_Note_ApplyB
	Apply C	🔲	ILS_L2_U2_Note_ApplyC
Speaking	Watch	🔲	ILS_L2_U2_Watch2
	Listen for Main Ideas	🔲	ILS_L2_U2_Watch2
	Apply B	🔲	ILS_L2_U2_Present_ApplyB
Pronunciation	Learn A	🔊	ILS_L2_U2_Pron_LearnA
	Learn B	🔊	ILS_L2_U2_Pron_LearnB
	Learn C	🔊	ILS_L2_U2_Pron_LearnC
	Apply A	🔊	ILS_L2_U2_Pron_ApplyA

UNIT 3

Listening	Listen	🔊	ILS_L2_U3_Listen1
	Listen for Main Ideas	🔊	ILS_L2_U3_Listen1
	Apply A	🔊	ILS_L2_U3_Listen_ApplyA
	Apply B	🔊	ILS_L2_U3_Listen_ApplyB
Speaking	Listen	🔊	ILS_L2_U3_Listen2
	Listen for Main Ideas	🔊	ILS_L2_U3_Listen2
	Apply B	🔊	ILS_L2_U3_Speak_ApplyB
Pronunciation	Learn A	🔊	ILS_L2_U3_Pron_LearnA
	Apply A	🔊	ILS_L2_U3_Pron_ApplyA
	Apply B	🔊	ILS_L2_U3_Pron_ApplyA
	Apply C	🔊	ILS_L2_U3_Pron_ApplyC
	Apply D	🔊	ILS_L2_U3_Pron_ApplyD
End of Unit Task	A	🔊	ILS_L2_U3_End

UNIT 4

Listening	Listen	🔊	ILS_L2_U4_Listen
	Listen for Main Ideas	🔊	ILS_L2_U4_Listen
	Apply A	🔊	ILS_L2_U4_Listen
Speaking	Watch	🔲	ILS_L2_U4_Watch
	Listen for Main Ideas	🔲	ILS_L2_U4_Watch
	Apply A	🔲	ILS_L2_U4_Watch
Pronunciation	Learn A	🔊	ILS_L2_U4_Pron_LearnA
	Learn B	🔊	ILS_L2_U4_Pron_LearnB
	Apply A	🔊	ILS_L2_U4_Pron_ApplyA

UNIT 5

Listening	Watch	🔲	ILS_L2_U5_Watch
	Listen for Main Ideas	🔲	ILS_L2_U5_Watch
	Apply A	🔲	ILS_L2_U5_Listen_ApplyA
	Apply B	🔲	ILS_L2_U5_Listen_ApplyB
Speaking	Listen	🔊	ILS_L2_U5_Listen
	Listen for Main Ideas	🔊	ILS_L2_U5_Listen
	Apply A	🔊	ILS_L2_U5_Listen
Pronunciation	Learn A	🔊	ILS_L2_U5_Pron_LearnA
	Learn B	🔊	ILS_L2_U5_Pron_LearnB
	Learn C	🔊	ILS_L2_U5_Pron_LearnC
	Apply A	🔊	ILS_L2_U5_Pron_ApplyA

UNIT 6

Listening	Listen	🔊	ILS_L2_U6_Listen1
	Listen for Main Ideas	🔊	ILS_L2_U6_Listen1
	Apply A	🔊	ILS_L2_U6_Listen1
Speaking	Listen	🔊	ILS_L2_U6_Listen2
	Listen for Main Ideas	🔊	ILS_L2_U6_Listen2
	Apply A	🔊	ILS_L2_U6_Present_ApplyA
	Apply B	🔊	ILS_L2_U6_Present_ApplyB
Pronunciation	Learn A	🔊	ILS_L2_U6_Pron_LearnA
	Learn B	🔊	ILS_L2_U6_Pron_LearnB
	Apply A	🔊	ILS_L2_U6_Pron_ApplyA
	Apply B	🔊	ILS_L2_U6_Pron_ApplyB

UNIT 7

Listening	Listen	🔊	ILS_L2_U7_Listen
	Listen for Main Ideas	🔊	ILS_L2_U7_Listen
	Apply A	🔊	ILS_L2_U7_Listen_ApplyA
	Apply B	🔊	ILS_L2_U7_Listen_ApplyB
Speaking	Watch	🔲	ILS_L2_U7_Watch
	Listen for Main Ideas	🔲	ILS_L2_U7_Watch
	Apply B	🔲	ILS_L2_U7_Watch
Pronunciation	Learn A	🔊	ILS_L2_U7_Pron_LearnA
	Learn B	🔊	ILS_L2_U7_Pron_LearnB
	Apply A	🔊	ILS_L2_U7_Pron_ApplyA

UNIT 8

Listening	Watch	🔲	ILS_L2_U8_Watch1
	Listen for Main Ideas	🔲	ILS_L2_U8_Watch1
	Apply B	🔲	ILS_L2_U8_Note_ApplyB
	Apply C	🔲	ILS_L2_U8_Note_ApplyC
Speaking	Watch	🔲	ILS_L2_U8_Watch2
	Listen for Main Ideas	🔲	ILS_L2_U8_Watch2
	Apply C	🔲	ILS_L2_U8_Watch2
Pronunciation	Learn A	🔊	ILS_L2_U8_Pron_LearnA
	Learn B	🔊	ILS_L2_U8_Pron_LearnB
	Learn C	🔊	ILS_L2_U8_Pron_LearnC
	Apply A	🔊	ILS_L2_U8_Pron_ApplyA
	Apply B	🔊	ILS_L2_U8_Pron_ApplyB

UNIT 9

Listening	Watch	🔲	ILS_L2_U9_Watch
	Listen for Main Ideas	🔲	ILS_L2_U9_Watch
	Apply B	🔲	ILS_L2_U9_Listen_ApplyB
Speaking	Listen	🔊	ILS_L2_U9_Listen
	Listen for Main Ideas	🔊	ILS_L2_U9_Listen
	Apply A	🔊	ILS_L2_U9_Listen
Pronunciation	Learn A	🔊	ILS_L2_U9_Pron_LearnA
	Learn B	🔊	ILS_L2_U9_Pron_LearnB
	Apply A	🔊	ILS_L2_U9_Pron_ApplyA
End of Unit Task	A	🔊	ILS_L2_U9_End

UNIT 10

Listening	Watch	🔲	ILS_L2_U10_Watch1
	Listen for Main Ideas	🔲	ILS_L2_U10_Watch1
	Apply A	🔲	ILS_L2_U10_Listen_ApplyA
Speaking	Watch	🔲	ILS_L2_U10_Watch2
	Listen for Main Ideas	🔲	ILS_L2_U10_Watch2
	Apply A	🔲	ILS_L2_U10_Present_ApplyA
	Apply B	🔲	ILS_L2_U10_Watch2
Pronunciation	Learn A	🔊	ILS_L2_U10_Pron_LearnA
	Learn B	🔊	ILS_L2_U10_Pron_LearnB
	Learn C	🔊	ILS_L2_U10_Pron_LearnC
	Apply A	🔊	ILS_L2_U10_Pron_ApplyA
	Apply B	🔊	ILS_L2_U10_Pron_ApplyB
	Apply C	🔊	ILS_L2_U10_Pron_ApplyC
End of Unit Task	A	🔊	ILS_L2_U10_End

OXFORD
UNIVERSITY PRESS

198 Madison Avenue

New York, NY 10016 USA

Great Clarendon Street, Oxford, OX2 6DP, United Kingdom

Oxford University Press is a department of the University of Oxford.
It furthers the University's objective of excellence in research, scholarship,
and education by publishing worldwide. Oxford is a registered trade
mark of Oxford University Press in the UK and in certain other countries

Adult Content Director: Stephanie Karras
Publisher: Sharon Sargent
Managing Editor: Tracey Gibbins
Senior Development Editor: Anna Norris
Associate Editor: Rachael Xerri
Head of Digital, Design, and Production: Bridget O'Lavin
Executive Art and Design Manager: Maj-Britt Hagsted
Content Production Manager: Julie Armstrong
Design Project Manager: Mary Chandler
Image Manager: Trisha Masterson

ISBN: 978 0 19 471924 7   STUDENT BOOK (PACK COMPONENT)
ISBN: 978 0 19 471923 0   STUDENT BOOK (PACK)
ISBN: 978 0 19 471921 6   WEBSITE (PACK COMPONENT)

Printed in China

This book is printed on paper from certified and well-managed sources

ACKNOWLEDGEMENTS

*We would also like to thank the following for permission to reproduce the following
photographs:* **Cover**, Robert Harding World Imagery/Alamy; Robert Preston
Photography/Alamy; Alex Ekins/Aurora Photos/Corbis; Fine Art Photographic
Library/Corbis; Iain Masterton/Getty Images; ValentynVolkov/istockphoto.
com; johnnychaos/istockphoto.com; Eliks/shutterstock.com. **Interior,** Alamy
pp. 16 (busy office/MBI), 25 (smart glasses/Rstudio), 32 (robotic arm/Mihajlo
Maricic), 40 (clock tower/roibu), 80 (collecting water/J Marshall/Tribaleye
Images), 104 (tablet capturing event/Jay Shaw-Baker); Corbis UK Ltd. p. 76
(examining a rock/Richard Baker/In Pictures); Getty Images pp. 4 (radar/
alengo), 13 (shared workspace/Ghislain & Marie David de Lossy), 28 (stock
movemen by smart glasses/Hiroshi Watanabe), 68 (energy food/Richard Jung),
73 (safety gear/Eduard Andras), 92 (tourist in China/Roberto Westbrook),
97 (Digital news/John Lamb), 100 (women using laptop/Zero Creatives), 109
(Illustration of vision/Dorling Kindersley), 116 (practicing Tai Chi/Lane Oatey/
Blue Jean Images); newscom.com p. 8 (revolving towers/CB2/ZOB/WENN);
Oxford University Press pp. 37 (Golden Eagle/Frank Burek), 112 (eye exam/
Stockbyte); Shutterstock pp. 4 (radar/alengo), 20 (skyscrapers in Dubai/S-F), 44
(hot air balloon/LittleStocker), 49 (ECO tree/Dragana Gerasimoski), 52 (view
from airplane/Richie Chan), 56 (students/wavebreakmedia), 61 (plate of food/
Alena Haurylik), 64 (diet plan/Rosabelverde), 85 (jewels on mannequin/Africa
Studio), 88 (shop window/Shcherbakov Ilya).

Acknowledgements

We would like to acknowledge the following individuals for their input during the development of the series:

Salam Affouneh
Higher Colleges of Technology
Abu Dhabi, U.A.E.

Kristin Bouton
Intensive English Institute
Illinois, U.S.A.

Nicole H. Carrasquel
Center for Multilingual Multicultural Studies
Florida, U.S.A.

Elaine Cockerham
Higher College of Technology
Muscat, Oman

Danielle Dilkes
CultureWorks English as a Second Language Inc.
Ontario, Canada

Susan Donaldson
Tacoma Community College
Washington, U.S.A

Penelope Doyle
Higher Colleges of Technology
Dubai, U.A.E.

Edward Roland Gray
Yonsei University
Seoul, South Korea

Melanie Golbert
Higher Colleges of Technology
Abu Dhabi, U.A.E.

Elise Harbin
Alabama Language Institute
Alabama, U.S.A.

Bill Hodges
University of Guelph
Ontario, Canada

David Daniel Howard
National Chiayi University
Chiayi

Leander Hughes
Saitama Daigaku
Saitama, Japan

James Ishler
Higher Colleges of Technology
Fujairah, U.A.E.

John Iveson
Sheridan College
Ontario, Canada

Alan Lanes
Higher Colleges of Technology
Dubai, U.A.E.

Corinne Marshall
Fanshawe College
Ontario, Canada

Christine Matta
College of DuPage
Illinois, U.S.A.

Beth Montag
University at Kearney
Nebraska, U.S.A.

Kevin Mueller
Tokyo International University
Saitama, Japan

Tracy Anne Munteanu
Higher Colleges of Technology
Fujairah, U.A.E.

Eileen O'Brien
Khalifa University of Science, Technology, and Research
Sharjah, U.A.E.

Jangyo Parsons
Kookmin University
Seoul, South Korea

John P. Racine
Dokkyo Daigaku
Soka City, Japan

Scott Rousseau
American University of Sharjah
Sharjah, U.A.E.

Jane Ryther
American River College
California, U.S.A

Kate Tindle
Zayed University
Dubai, U.A.E.

Melody Traylor
Higher Colleges of Technology
Fujairah, U.A.E.

John Vogels
Higher Colleges of Technology
Dubai, U.A.E.

Kelly Wharton
Fanshawe College
Ontario, Canada

Contents

MEDIA TRACK LIST i

ACKNOWLEDGEMENTS iii

THE INSIDE TRACK TO ACADEMIC SUCCESS vi

Unit 1 Solving a Mystery   1

Content Area: Engineering

LISTENING AND SPEAKING SKILLS: Cause and Effect Relationships;
Facilitating Group Discussions 4, 8

Pronunciation: *Intonation and Chunking Sentences* 10

Vocabulary activities 2, 6

Unit 2 A Marketplace of Ideas   13

Content Area: Business

LISTENING AND SPEAKING SKILLS: Abbreviations and Symbols;
Supporting Opinions 16, 21

Pronunciation: *Stress in Numbers* 22

Vocabulary activities 14, 18

Unit 3 Enhancing Reality   25

Content Area: Technology

LISTENING AND SPEAKING SKILLS: Signal Phrases; Sharing Opinions Politely 28, 32

Pronunciation: *Sentence Stress* 34

Vocabulary activities 26, 30

Unit 4 Literary Symbols   37

Content Area: Literature

LISTENING AND SPEAKING SKILLS: Outlining Notes;
Giving Short Oral Summaries 40, 44

Pronunciation: *Dropping the /h/ Sound* 46

Vocabulary activities 38, 42

Unit 5 Creative Solutions   49

Content Area: Meteorology

LISTENING AND SPEAKING SKILLS: Listening for Proposals;
Giving and Responding to Proposals 53, 56

Pronunciation: *Pronouncing Nasal Sounds* 58

Vocabulary activities 50, 54

Unit 6 What to Eat 61

Content Area: Nutrition

**LISTENING AND SPEAKING SKILLS: The Cornell Method to Take Notes;
Preparing Well-Organized Presentations** 64, 68

Pronunciation: *Dropping Syllables* 70

Vocabulary activities 62, 66

Unit 7 Working in the Field 73

Content Area: Geology

**LISTENING AND SPEAKING SKILLS: Listening for Implications;
Polite Requests and Interruptions** 76, 80

Pronunciation: *Three-Word Phrasal Verbs* 82

Vocabulary activities 74, 78

Unit 8 The Happiness Formula 85

Content Area: Sociology

**LISTENING AND SPEAKING SKILLS: Using Mind Maps;
Checking for Understanding** 89, 92

Pronunciation: *The /h/ Sound in Auxiliary Verbs* 94

Vocabulary activities 86, 90

Unit 9 Stop the Presses 97

Content Area: Journalism

**LISTENING AND SPEAKING SKILLS: Facts and Opinions;
Being Persuasive in Academic Discussions** 100, 104

Pronunciation: *Common Reductions* 106

Vocabulary activities 98, 102

Unit 10 Artificial Retina 109

Content Area: Medicine

**LISTENING AND SPEAKING SKILLS: Using Context to Follow a Lecture;
Nonverbal Communication** 113, 116

Pronunciation: *Contrastive and Emphatic Stress* 118

Vocabulary activities 110, 114

INDEX: ACADEMIC WORD LIST 121

The Inside Track to Academic Success

Student Books

For additional student resources, visit: www.insidelisteningandspeaking.com.

iTools for all levels

The *Inside Listening and Speaking* iTools component is for use with a projector or interactive whiteboard.

Resources for whole-class presentation

> **Book-on-screen** focuses class on teaching points and facilitates classroom management.

> **Audio and video** at point of use facilitates engaging, dynamic lessons.

Resources for assessment and preparation

> Customizable Unit, Mid-term, and Final Tests evaluate student progress.

> Complete Answer Keys are provided.

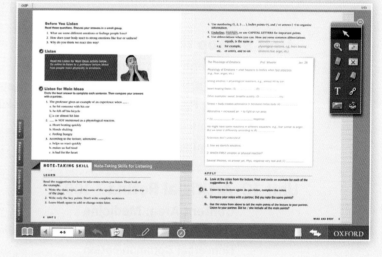

For additional instructor resources, visit: www.oup.com/elt/teacher/insidelisteningandspeaking.

About *Inside Listening and Speaking*

Unit features

> **Explicit skills instruction** prepares students for academic listening

> **Authentic videos** from a variety of academic contexts engage and motivate students

> **Pronunciation instruction** ensures students are articulate, clear speakers

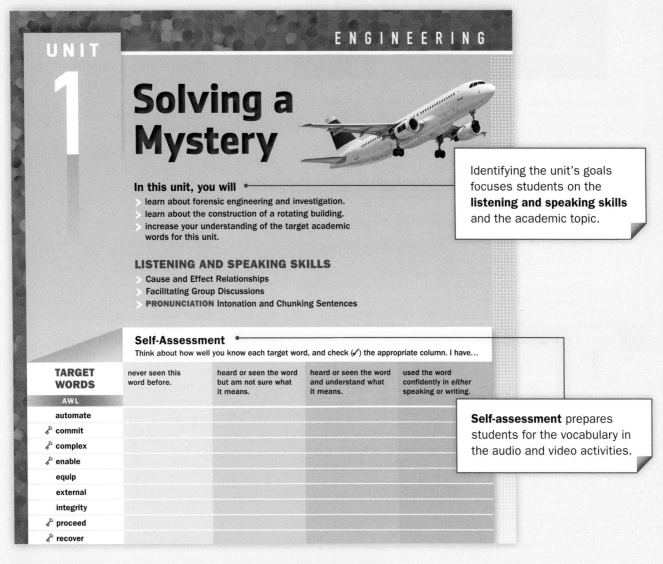

ENGINEERING

UNIT 1

Solving a Mystery

In this unit, you will
> learn about forensic engineering and investigation.
> learn about the construction of a rotating building.
> increase your understanding of the target academic words for this unit.

LISTENING AND SPEAKING SKILLS
> Cause and Effect Relationships
> Facilitating Group Discussions
> **PRONUNCIATION** Intonation and Chunking Sentences

Identifying the unit's goals focuses students on the **listening and speaking skills** and the academic topic.

Self-Assessment

Think about how well you know each target word, and check (✓) the appropriate column. I have...

TARGET WORDS	never seen this word before.	heard or seen the word but am not sure what it means.	heard or seen the word and understand what it means.	used the word confidently in *either* speaking or writing.
AWL				
automate				
🔑 commit				
🔑 complex				
🔑 enable				
equip				
external				
integrity				
🔑 proceed				
🔑 recover				

Self-assessment prepares students for the vocabulary in the audio and video activities.

The Academic Word List and the Oxford 3000

Based on a corpus of 4.3 million words, the **Academic Word List (AWL)** is the most principled and widely accepted list of academic words. Compiled by Averil Coxhead in 2000, it was informed by academic materials across the academic disciplines.

The **Oxford 3000™** have been carefully selected by a group of language experts and experienced teachers as the most important and useful words to learn in English. The Oxford 3000 are based on the American English section of the Oxford English Corpus.

Oxford 3000 and Academic Word List vocabulary is integrated throughout the unit and practiced in context through audio and video resources.

Explicit Skills Instruction

Before You Listen

Read these questions. Discuss your answers in a small group.

1. Do you think it is safer to travel by car, by train, or by airplane? Why?
2. Do you think a well-trained pilot or a high-tech automated flight system is more important for flight safety? Why?
3. What was your most memorable travel experience?

> **Discussion questions activate students' knowledge** and prepare them to listen.

Listen

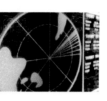

Read the Listen for Main Ideas activity below. Go online to listen to engineer Alex Edward give a talk at an aviation safety conference on Flight 447's mysterious disappearance.

Listen for Main Ideas

Read the statements about the audio. Circle the best answer to complete each sentence.

1. The plane's external speed sensors ___.
   a. were broken
   b. were damaged by lightning
   c. were frozen
2. Speed data is needed for the plane's ___ to work properly.
   a. automated systems
   b. external parts
   c. internal engines
3. After taking manual control, the pilots did not know their speed, and they ___.
   a. slowed the plane too quickly
   b. increased the plane's speed too much
   c. returned to automated systems
4. Alex Edward says that engineers must be committed to ___.
   a. developing new investigative methods
   b. improving design and safety
   c. improving manual controls

> **Comprehension activities** help students understand the listening materials in preparation for academic skills instruction.

LISTENING SKILL — Cause and Effect Relationships

LEARN

A cause makes something happen. An effect is the result of a cause.

| Cause: wanted to work overseas | → | Effect: applied for a job with an international company |

*The student wanted to work overseas, **so** he applied for a job with an international company.*

> **Listening and speaking skill instruction** is linked to the academic content. **Apply** sections give students the opportunity to practice the skills in context.

APPLY

A. Work with a partner. Using the cause and effect signal phrases, discuss different sentences that you can make with the phrases below.

1. study hard / be able to pass the exam (because / so)

   Because she studied hard, she was able to pass the exam.

   She studied hard, so she was able to pass the exam.

2. have internship experience / be a good person for the job (since / as a result)
3. get a part-time job / be able to save money for a trip overseas (so / because)

B. Go online to listen to part of the audio again, and complete the chart below.

Cause	Effect
1. ... **because** the plane had traveled through ... _super-cooled water_	1. On the outside of the plane, the speed sensors had frozen ...
2. ... the plane's automated systems were not getting necessary speed data.	2. **As a result,** _____ _____ ...
3. ... **because** these _____	3. the pilots decided to [take manual] control of the plane.

High-Interest Media Content

Before You Watch

Read these questions. Discuss your answers in a small group.

1. Would you prefer to work for a small company or a large company? Why?
2. What are some of the world's most interesting new companies? How have they changed our world?
3. What are some of the difficulties people face when starting a new business?

Watch

Read the Listen for Main Ideas activity below. Go online to watch a businesswoman talk about shared workspaces and how they are helping new businesses achieve success. She also gives advice for future entrepreneurs.

Listen for Main Ideas

Read the questions about the video. Work with a partner to ask and answer these questions.

1. What is a shared workspace?
2. Why do new, small businesses use shared workspaces?
3. How does this entrepreneur find new customers?
4. What advice does she give other entrepreneurs?

NOTE-TAKING SKILL   Abbreviations and Symbols

LEARN

During a lecture, you should take notes on 1) main ideas, 2) supporting information, and 3) key words. Do not try to write down every word you hear. In your notes, ignore grammar rules and write only key words.

People hear about us from their friends, co-workers, other people they know. We do coordinate social events and "Networking Nights," though, which have helped us find new customers.

> Notes: Find new customers—people's friends / co-workers, social events, networking

16   UNIT 2

Audio and video including lectures, professional presentations, classroom discussions, and student presentations expose students to a **variety of academic contexts**.

High-interest, original academic video and authentic BBC content motivate students.

Pronunciation Instruction

Pronunciation skill instruction is supported by audio resources to ensure students are articulate, clear speakers.

PRONUNCIATION SKILL | Intonation and Chunking Sentences

LEARN

Intonation is the rise and fall of speech. Falling intonation occurs at the end of statements and *wh-* questions. Rising intonation occurs at the end of *yes / no* questions.

Chunking, or separating words into meaningful groups by pausing (|), also has its own intonation.

A. Go online to listen to the sentences. Notice the rising or falling intonation at the end of each sentence.

1. Engineers recommended making the concrete core thicker.
2. What about green technology?
3. Has everyone done the reading?

Students **learn and apply** pronunciation skills in the context of the academic topic.

B. You break sentences into chunks by pausing (|). Each chunk has a focus word. This is the most important word in that chunk. The chunks have rising intonation, except the last chunk in a statement or *wh-* question.

Go online to listen. Notice the intonation in each chunk. The focus words are in pink.

1. It's going to be the first rotating skyscraper | after it is completed.
2. What's so interesting | about this building?
3. Are we missing anything | related to the building's green technology?
4. The units will be built completely finished | with air-conditioning, | flooring, | and lighting.
5. Are you interested in green technology, | construction, | and modern architecture?

APPLY

A. Go online to listen to the sentences. Draw a line (|) to separate the sentences into chunks. Draw arrows to show rising or falling intonation. Underline the focus word. Then say the sentences aloud with the appropriate pausing and intonation.

1. Experts looked | at the plane's air traffic control records | for answers.
2. Previously, the Airbus 330 model had had no accidents and very few serious problems.
3. What are some aspects of this building that make it unique, unusual, or complex?

UNIT 1

Solving a Mystery

In this unit, you will

> learn about forensic engineering and investigation.
> learn about the construction of a rotating building.
> increase your understanding of the target academic words for this unit.

LISTENING AND SPEAKING SKILLS

> Cause and Effect Relationships
> Facilitating Group Discussions
> PRONUNCIATION Intonation and Chunking Sentences

Self-Assessment

Think about how well you know each target word, and check (✓) the appropriate column. I have…

TARGET WORDS	never seen this word before.	heard or seen the word but am not sure what it means.	heard or seen the word and understand what it means.	used the word confidently in *either* speaking or writing.
AWL				
automate				
🔑 commit				
🔑 complex				
🔑 enable				
equip				
external				
integrity				
🔑 proceed				
🔑 recover				
🔑 reveal				
🔑 structure				
🔑 vary				

🔑 Oxford 3000™ keywords

Vocabulary Activities

Word Form Chart		
Noun	**Verb**	**Adjective**
automation	automate	automated automatic
commitment	commit	committed
equipment	equip	equipped
recovery	recover	recoverable

A. Complete the paragraph below using the correct form of the target words in the Word Form Chart.

Most big airlines are _____*committed*_____ to improving the quality
(1. willing to give time to something)

and comfort of their flights. For example, to help passengers make a quicker

_____ from long international flights, many
(2. return to health)

airlines are using seats that can become beds. Newer planes are also being

_____ with _____ seats
(3. supplied)   (4. operated without direct human control)

that change based on a passenger's body size and movements. This new

technological _____ improves both safety and
(5. machinery)

comfort through _____ .
(6. the use of machines)

B. The word *automate* means "to use machines and computers instead of people
to do a job or task." Rank each automated activity or item in the chart below
(1 = the most, 4 = the least). Compare your answers with a partner's.

Activity or item	Usefulness	Importance to people in general
automated guided vehicles		
automated teller machines (ATM)		
automated surgical robots		
automated phone services		

C. *External* means "connected with or located on the outside of something." Match
the items at the top of page 3 with where you would find them.

<u>d</u> 1. external headlights
___ 2. external light sensor
___ 3. external links
___ 4. external hard drive
___ 5. external parking lot security cameras
___ 6. external stairway

a. on the outside of a house
b. on the outside of a computer
c. on the outside of a large store
d. on the outside of a car
e. on the outside of a building
f. to the outside of a website

D. *Reveal* **means "to make something known." Complete the sentences below with the phrases from the box. One phrase will be used twice.**

the cause of	her plans to	a connection between	the plane's	his interest in

1. The investigation revealed _____*the cause of*_____ the accident.

2. The customers' answers revealed _____ the new product, which excited the sales team.

3. Our research reveals _____ the two groups. Group A affects Group B positively.

4. In an email, she revealed _____ stop working at the end of the year.

5. Error warnings revealed that _____ automated systems stopped working during the flight.

6. The medical tests revealed _____ the patient's illness.

E. **Write the letter that best matches the meaning of** *recover* **in each sentence.**

a. to regain something that was lost or stolen	c. to become well after being sick
b. to get back to normal after a bad experience	d. to get back the use of senses

<u>c</u> 1. After one week in the hospital, he made a full recovery.
___ 2. She recovered her hearing after the operation.
___ 3. Most members of the team took a long time to recover after losing the championship match.
___ 4. The police were able to recover the stolen items.
___ 5. It took the student almost a week to recover from the illness.
___ 6. The child recovered his backpack after a woman found it on the bus.
___ 7. The speaker hoped to recover his voice after several days of relaxation.

About the Topic

Forensic engineers study materials, structures, and products when they fail. After a disaster, the engineers try to determine what went wrong to avoid future accidents. For example, when a plane crashes, they investigate the parts of the plane, air traffic control records, and the plane's automated systems.

Before You Listen

Read these questions. Discuss your answers in a small group.

1. Do you think it is safer to travel by car, by train, or by airplane? Why?
2. Do you think a well-trained pilot or a high-tech automated flight system is more important for flight safety? Why?
3. What was your most memorable travel experience?

Listen

Read the Listen for Main Ideas activity below. Go online to listen to engineer Alex Edward give a talk at an aviation safety conference on Flight 447's mysterious disappearance.

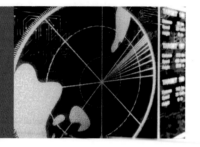

Listen for Main Ideas

Read the statements about the audio. Circle the best answer to complete each sentence.

1. The plane's external speed sensors ___.
   a. were broken
   b. were damaged by lightning
   c. were frozen
2. Speed data is needed for the plane's ___ to work properly.
   a. automated systems
   b. external parts
   c. internal engines
3. After taking manual control, the pilots did not know their speed, and they ___.
   a. slowed the plane too quickly
   b. increased the plane's speed too much
   c. returned to automated systems
4. Alex Edward says that engineers must be committed to ___.
   a. developing new investigative methods
   b. improving design and safety
   c. improving manual controls

LISTENING SKILL | Cause and Effect Relationships

LEARN

A cause makes something happen. An effect is the result of a cause.

Cause: wanted to work overseas	→	Effect: applied for a job with an international company

*The student wanted to work overseas, **so** he applied for a job with an international company.*

In lectures, presentations, and discussions, speakers often talk about cause and effect relationships to show connections between important points. Look at the signal phrases in the charts below that show cause and effect relationships.

Cause signal phrases (reason)
Because / Since he applied for the job, he was called for an interview.
Because of his work experience, he got the job.
Speakers may also place cause signal phrases in the middle of a sentence.
He was called for an interview **because / since** he had work experience.
He got the job **because of** his work experience.

Effect signal phrases (result)
He had a lot of experience. **As a result / Therefore**, he was called for an interview.
He had a lot of experience, **so** he was called for an interview.

APPLY

A. Work with a partner. Using the cause and effect signal phrases, discuss different sentences that you can make with the phrases below.

1. study hard / be able to pass the exam (because / so)

   Because she studied hard, she was able to pass the exam.

   *She studied hard, **so** she was able to pass the exam.*

2. have internship experience / be a good person for the job (since / as a result)

3. get a part-time job / be able to save money for a trip overseas (so / because)

B. Go online to listen to part of the audio again, and complete the chart below.

Cause	Effect
1. ... **because** the plane had traveled through ... <u>super-cooled water</u>	1. On the outside of the plane, the speed sensors had frozen ...
2. ... the plane's automated systems were not getting necessary speed data.	2. **As a result,** _____ _____ ...
3. ... **because** these _____ _____ ,	3. the pilots decided to [take manual] control of the plane.

C. Go online to listen to the last part of the audio. Use signal words to discuss the following cause and effect relationships with your partner.

1. external speed sensors, frozen → pilots did not know speed

2. pilots slowed plane too quickly → plane fell and crashed

SPEAKING

Vocabulary Activities

The noun *structure* sometimes refers to a building.

> We've been studying how large **structures** can produce green energy.

Structure may also refer to "the way in which the parts of something are connected together, arranged, or organized."

> The **structure** of the university consists of nine colleges. Under each college, there are several departments.

CORPUS

A. Write the letter that best matches the correct meaning of *structure* in each sentence.

> a. the design / organization of something   b. a building

___b___ 1. The new structure downtown has a traditional design.

_____ 2. The structure of the company meant that most employees worked in teams.

_____ 3. The structure for the course enabled the professor to cover the entire book.

_____ 4. One of the oldest structures in town is the railway station.

_____ 5. The molecule's structures was more complex than scientists had thought.

As an adjective, *complex* means "difficult to understand."

> You must do many **complex** problems in physics class.

Complex also refers to things "made of many different things or parts that are connected."

> The subway system is **complex**. It connects 20 different lines and 200 stations underground.

As a noun, *complex* refers to "a group of buildings of a similar type together in one place."

> The factory was only a small part of a larger **complex** that served the community.

CORPUS

B. Keeping the definitions of *complex* in mind, fill out the chart below. Share your answers with a partner.

Academic subjects that are complex	Group of connected structures that are often complexes	Systems or designs that are complex
1. *physics*	1. *factories*	1. *subway systems*
2.	2.	2.
3.	3.	3.

C. Write a form of the target word from the box that works best for each of the phrases below.

enable	proceed	structure	vary

1. The group ___*proceeded*___ with a plan.
              with the second part of the presentation.

2. The new technology _____ the team to complete the project faster.
              the company to sell its products online.

3. The manager _____ the department with five teams.
              a meeting around five problems.

4. Universities _____ in size.
              in quality.

D. *Structural integrity* refers to "the strength of a building." How important are the following to the structural integrity of a building? Discuss your answers with a partner.

	Not important	Somewhat important	Very important
The design of the building		✓	
The materials used in the construction of the building			
The environmental conditions around the building			
The number of workers used to construct the building			

About the Topic

A rotating building is one that moves or turns around a central core. Many cities have buildings with a rotating top floor. The Suite Vollard in Brazil was the first completely rotating building. Similar projects are underway in Dubai and Moscow.

Before You Listen

Read these questions. Discuss your answers in a small group.

1. Which famous buildings or structures do you find interesting or unique?

2. Do you prefer traditional or modern architectural designs?

3. Have you ever seen or been in a rotating building?

Listen

Read the Listen for Main Ideas activity below. Go online to listen to Dr. Robert Wang lead a group discussion in a structural engineering class. Dr. Wang talks about the world's first rotating tower and how its separately rotating floors will be constructed.

Listen for Main Ideas

Mark each sentence as *T* (true) or *F* (false). Work with a partner. Restate false sentences to make them correct.

___F___ 1. The building's floors turn together at one time. *The floors turn separately.*

_____ 2. The floors of the building will be made in a factory.

_____ 3. It will take a very long time to complete the building.

_____ 4. The central concrete core will ensure the integrity of building.

SPEAKING SKILL   Facilitating Group Discussions

LEARN

In class, you may be asked to have group discussions. It is important that everyone speaks and participates. In the audio, Dr. Wang is the facilitator. He keeps the conversation moving and includes everyone in the discussion. The chart below has skills and language you will need to facilitate a discussion.

Facilitation skills	Phrases
1. Introducing the Discussion	Maybe we could begin with … Should we get started? *Why don't we start with …*
2. Guiding the Discussion	Let's move on to … We can always come back to it later.
3. Providing Positive Encouragement	That's a great idea. That's a good point.

4. Ensuring Group Participation	What do you think about what she just said? What do you think? _____
5. Closing the Discussion	So, have we covered everything? Let's summarize before we finish. _____

APPLY

A. Add these phrases to the correct facilitation skills in the chart above.

Why don't we start with …	What's your opinion?	That makes perfect sense.
For next time, let's …	Can we review the second point now?	

B. Work with a partner. What expressions can you use for each situation?

1. Bob has not said a word for almost ten minutes, but he is listening.

   Bob, what do you think about her idea?

2. The group has just finished discussing the final homework question.

3. One member of your group thinks of a new idea for your group project.

C. Read the phrases below. Listen to the audio again and fill in the blanks.

Facilitation skills	Phrases
1. Introducing the Discussion	OK, should we _____?
2. Guiding the Discussion	OK, now why don't _____. What about green technology?
3. Providing Positive Encouragement	That means they'll save money, too. That's a _____.
4. Ensuring Group Participation	What _____, Gary?
5. Closing the Discussion	Exactly. OK, so let's _____ …

D. Work in a small group and discuss one of the topics below. Assign facilitation skills to each member of the group.

- Professional athletes earn too much money.
- Universities should require foreign language classes.
- Smoking should not be allowed on university campuses.

PRONUNCIATION SKILL   Intonation and Chunking Sentences

LEARN

Intonation is the rise and fall of speech. Falling intonation occurs at the end of statements and *wh-* questions. Rising intonation occurs at the end of *yes / no* questions.

Chunking, or separating words into meaningful groups by pausing (|), also has its own intonation.

A. Go online to listen to the sentences. Notice the rising or falling intonation at the end of each sentence.

1. Engineers recommended making the concrete core thicker.
2. What about green technology?
3. Has everyone done the reading?

You break sentences into chunks by pausing (|). Each chunk has a focus word. This is the most important word in that chunk. The chunks have rising intonation, except the last chunk in a statement or *wh-* question.

B. Go online to listen. Notice the intonation in each chunk. The focus words are in pink.

1. It's going to be the first rotating skyscraper | after it is completed.
2. What's so interesting | about this building?
3. Are we missing anything | related to the building's green technology?
4. The units will be built completely finished | with air-conditioning, | flooring, | and lighting.
5. Are you interested in green technology, | construction, | and modern architecture?

APPLY

A. Go online to listen to the sentences. Draw a line (|) to separate the sentences into chunks. Draw arrows to show rising or falling intonation. Underline the focus word. Then say the sentences aloud with the appropriate pausing and intonation.

1. Experts looked | at the plane's air traffic control records | for answers.
2. Previously, the Airbus 330 model had had no accidents and very few serious problems.
3. What are some aspects of this building that make it unique, unusual, or complex?

B. With a partner, ask about the causes and effects of some everyday decisions. Use appropriate intonation and pausing.

> A: What is the effect | of doing all of your assignments electronically?
>
> B: Since I do all of my assignments electronically, | I can save them on my computer | and keep them forever.
>
> A: Do you think this will help for the classes you take | in the future?
>
> B: Yes, I do.

End of Unit Task

In this unit, you learned how to listen for and use language to describe cause and effect relationships. You also learned how to facilitate group discussions. Review these skills by taking notes on a new audio about the positive and negative effects of a landfill project. Then discuss the landfill project, using the facilitation skills that you learned.

A. Discuss the following questions in small groups.

1. What is a landfill?
2. What are some reasons why governments build landfills?

B. Go online to listen to engineer Sarah Stewart discuss the positive effects of the landfill project. Complete the notes. Then compare your answers in small groups.

Cause	Effect
1. (**because**) won't have to pay other cities	1. _enable us to save money_
2. recover gas from waste	2. (**so**) decrease _____
3. one of the safest ways to store garbage	3. (**as a result**) limit _____

C. Go online to listen to engineer Frank Yamato discuss the negative effects of the landfill project. Complete the notes. Then compare your answers in small groups.

Cause	Effect
1. (**because**) many homes near the landfill	1. _live with smells, chemicals_
2. landfill site close to water source	2. (**as a result**) landfill could pollute _____
3. (**since**) a big project	3. cost a lot of money and take _____

D. Work in groups of five. Discuss whether your group would build the landfill or not. Assign facilitator roles to each student (skills 1–5 from pages 8–9). As you make your decision, discuss the causes and effects related to building the landfill.

Self-Assessment		
Yes	**No**	
☐	☐	I successfully identified cause and effect relationships.
☐	☐	I successfully participated in the group discussion.
☐	☐	I successfully used facilitation skills during the group discussion.
☐	☐	I can speak with accurate intonation.
☐	☐	I can correctly use the target vocabulary words from the unit.

Discussion Questions

With a partner or in a small group, discuss the following questions.

1. What can governments do to ensure that airplanes and buildings have structural integrity?

2. What problems could arise from a rotating building?

3. Should an architect focus on the practical uses of a building or on making it attractive and interesting?

UNIT 2

A Marketplace of Ideas

In this unit, you will

> learn about shared workspaces and other ideas for improving business.
> increase your understanding of the target academic words for this unit.

LISTENING AND SPEAKING SKILLS

> Abbreviations and Symbols
> Supporting Opinions
> **PRONUNCIATION** Stress in Numbers

Self-Assessment

Think about how well you know each target word, and check (✓) the appropriate column. I have...

TARGET WORDS	never seen this word before.	heard or seen the word but am not sure what it means.	heard or seen the word and understand what it means.	used the word confidently in *either* speaking or writing.
AWL				
🔑 authority				
🔑 cease				
converse				
coordinate				
evolve				
mutual				
🔑 network				
preliminary				
🔑 region				
regulate				
🔑 strategy				
🔑 style				

🔑 Oxford 3000™ keywords

LISTENING

Vocabulary Activities

A. Cross out the word or phrase in parentheses with a different meaning from the others. Use a dictionary to help you understand new words. Compare answers with a partner.

1. It was in their (*common / expert / shared / mutual*) interest to work together, so the two companies collaborated on the project.

2. The (*evolution of / development of / decline in / advancement of*) technology has created new opportunities for young entrepreneurs.

3. Because they (*talk with / meet with / speak to / converse with*) other small business owners, they can share new ideas.

4. The company (*coordinated / organized / planned / visited*) a networking event. A networking event is an event for people to meet, talk, and share information with one another.

5. The (*preliminary work / work that must be completed first / preparatory work / typical work*) is not finished, so the investigation cannot start.

6. Their department made a / an (*basic / stylish / fashionable / attractive*) new design.

The verb *coordinate* means "to organize [something] … so that it works well." The noun form is *coordination*.

> *(1) The* **coordination** *of the meeting was done by the director.*

Coordination also refers to "choosing colors that look nice together, for example, in clothes or furniture."

> *(2) The stylist was responsible for the* **coordination** *of the actor's clothing.*

The word can also mean "the ability to control your movements well."

> *(3) Good hand* **coordination** *is important when playing a musical instrument.*

 CORPUS

B. Using the definitions above, list different phrases related to each meaning (1–3) of *coordination*. Discuss your answers with a partner.

Coordination (1)	Coordination (2)	Coordination (3)
1. *a school event*	1. *a shirt and tie*	1. *basketball*
2. _____	2. _____	2. _____
3. _____	3. _____	3. _____

C. Write *M* (*mutual* interest) beside activities that you and another person or group benefit from working on together. Write *I* (independent) beside activities that are best done independently. Then add and label two of your own activities.

_I_ 1. deciding professional goals   ___ 5. preparing for an exam

___ 2. deciding which classes to take   ___ 6. taking notes in class

___ 3. preparing for a job interview   ___ 7. writing a research paper

___ 4. _____   ___ 8. _____

D. Interview a partner. Fill out the chart based on your partner's answers.

Questions	Partner's answers
1. Networking is when you try to meet or talk to people who may be helpful to you in your work. What is one job that requires a lot of networking?	
2. A network is a system of roads and lines that cross and connect to each other. What transportation or machines operate on a network?	
3. A network also refers to a group of television stations that broadcast the same programs at the same time. What is your favorite television network?	

E. *Cease* means "to stop." Complete the sentences with the phrases in the box.

ceased to exist	ceased operations	never ceased to amaze
ceased to be true	ceased to be a member	

1. There are no more Dodo birds in the world. The bird ___ceased to exist___ in the late 1600s.

2. The instructor always had very interesting lectures. She _____ her students.

3. He was in our study group, but he _____ after he moved.

4. Students received scholarships to study abroad, but that _____ after the university stopped giving money to the scholarship program.

5. The factory closed and _____ after having been open for thirty years.

About the Topic

To save on costs, more and more business owners are sharing office space. By renting shared space with other businesses, entrepreneurs can invest their money in starting their new companies rather than in the costs of desks and machinery. Even conference rooms and equipment can be rented through shared office space.

Before You Watch

Read these questions. Discuss your answers in a small group.

1. Would you prefer to work for a small company or a large company? Why?

2. What are some of the world's most interesting new companies? How have they changed our world?

3. What are some of the difficulties people face when starting a new business?

Watch

Read the Listen for Main Ideas activity below. Go online to watch a businesswoman talk about shared workspaces and how they are helping new businesses achieve success. She also gives advice for future entrepreneurs.

Listen for Main Ideas

Read the questions about the video. Work with a partner to ask and answer these questions.

1. What is a shared workspace?

2. Why do new, small businesses use shared workspaces?

3. How does this entrepreneur find new customers?

4. What advice does she give other entrepreneurs?

NOTE-TAKING SKILL Abbreviations and Symbols

LEARN

During a lecture, you should take notes on 1) main ideas, 2) supporting information, and 3) key words. Do not try to write down every word you hear. In your notes, ignore grammar rules and write only key words.

People hear about us from their friends, co-workers, other people they know. We do coordinate social events and "Networking Nights," though, which have helped us find new customers.

> Notes: *Find new customers—people's friends / co-workers, social events, networking*

Use symbols and abbreviations in your notes.

Word	Abbreviation	Word	Symbol
with, without	w/, w/o	equal / not equal, is / is not	= ≠
because	b/c	increase / decrease	↑↓
and so on	etc.	causes / becomes	→
for example	e.g.	and	+
question, answer	Q, A	important	★

You know, new businesses often cease to exist because of the high rent for office space. So our cheaper shared rental space gives new businesses a chance to succeed during the preliminary stages of their development.

Notes: *New biz—close b/c high rent → shared space = chance to succeed*

APPLY

A. Add at least two symbols or abbreviations that you use when taking notes into the chart above. Compare your abbreviations and symbols with a partner.

B. Go online to watch the first part of the interview. Take notes using abbreviations and symbols. Compare your notes with those of a partner.

So, could you tell our listeners what a shared workspace is?	*shared wk. space = open office, share ideas + info., etc.*
How did you get the idea to open a shared workspace?	_____ told about shared wkspace, her city
What kinds of companies rent space from you?	wide range—e.g. tech, fashion, _____

C. Watch another part of the interview. As you watch the video, take notes using simple language, abbreviations, and symbols.

Do you do anything to find new customers?	coordinate → _____
What are your plans for the future?	_____

D. Work with a partner. Using your notes, take turns discussing with a partner the answers to the questions from activities B and C.

Vocabulary Activities

Word Form Chart		
Noun	**Adjective**	**Adverb**
region	regional	regionally
regulation regulator	regulatory	_____
strategy	strategic	strategically

A. Complete the paragraph below using the correct form of the target words in the Word Form Chart.

The government made a ___strategic___ decision to invest in infrastructure.
  (1. planned)

As a result, the airport has become a center for travel in the _____.
  (2. area)

Additionally, several international companies have moved their _____
  (3. local area)

offices to the city because of its large shipping port. The port can move

freight and containers quickly. In the city, there are free zones. Each free zone

has a governing authority and _____.
  (4. organization that makes rules)

B. Complete the sentences using the correct form of the target words from the Word Form Chart above.

1. The new ___regulation___ helped to improve air quality.
   (rule)

2. The team developed a _____ for increasing sales.
   (plan)

3. The _____ saw an increase in tourism.
   (area)

4. The _____ office decreased controls on banks.
   (rule-making)

C. *Region* can refer to "one of the areas that a country is divided into." Work with a partner. Discuss different things that can vary from region to region within a country. Use *regional* + noun.

1. ___regional food___   3. _____

2. _____   4. _____

D. The word *authority* refers to a group of people or an organization that has the power to make decisions in a particular area. Fill out the chart below. Compare your answers with a partner.

Does your university have:	Yes / No	If yes, rank the governing authority's performance (1 = poor, 5 = excellent)
a governing authority for the entire university?		
a student-led governing authority?		
a governing authority for health and safety?		
a governing authority for campus housing?		

The verb *regulate* means "to control something by means of rules."

*I think the government should **regulate** air pollution caused by factories.*

A *regulation* is "an official rule" that controls how something is done.

*These **regulations** would help reduce air pollution.*

CORPUS

E. For each category below, how much government regulation would you prefer?

The government ...	Should regulate	Should regulate slightly	Should not regulate
Air and water pollution from factories and businesses	✓		
The kinds of subjects that high schools must teach all students			
The amount of CEO pay and income			
The number of calories allowed in fast food			
The price of gas and electricity			

About the Topic

City planners need to make strategic decisions on how to invest in infrastructure or whether to create economic free zones. Infrastructure refers to the systems and services that help a city run smoothly. For example, airports, shipping ports, subway systems, and roads are parts of a city's infrastructure. An economic free zone is an area where there are little or no taxes.

Before You Watch

Read these questions. Discuss your answers in a small group.

1. What do you think makes a city good for doing business?

2. Which cities are international centers for business?

3. What contributes most to a city's quality of life? Is it schools, public transportation, housing, green space, or something else?

Watch

Read the Listen for Main Ideas activity below. Go online to watch a presentation on doing business in Dubai. The presentation talks about how the city became one of the world's centers for business and how it continues to move forward today.

Listen for Main Ideas

Mark each sentence as *T* (true) or *F* (false). Work with a partner. Restate false sentences to make them correct.

___*F*___ 1. Dubai's oil industry is responsible for most of its economy.

      Dubai's leaders expanded the economic focus with infrastructure and free zones.

_____ 2. Dubai is a center for shipping in the region.

_____ 3. Chinese companies have moved to Dubai to trade with the Middle East.

_____ 4. The free zones have small corporate and personal income taxes.

_____ 5. Dubai needs better hospitals and schools.

PRESENTATION SKILL   Supporting Opinions

LEARN

In class, you will often be asked to present your opinion on a discussion topic. Giving only your opinion, however, is often not enough. Supporting your opinion with facts and statistics will make your opinion stronger.

Opinion: Dubai is the most important center for shipping in the Middle East.

Support:

• **Fact:** Many Chinese companies have moved to Dubai to trade with the Middle East.

• **Fact:** Cargo from Dubai goes to Bahrain, Kuwait, Doha, and Abu Dhabi.

• **Statistic:** 850 countries do business at the port in Dubai.

A fact is information that you can prove. A statistic is a number that shows a fact.

A. Look at the statements below. Working with a partner, discuss two or three kinds of statistical or factual support that you could use for each statement.

The city has a growing tourism industry.	• Show that the numbers of tourists visiting the city has increased. • List the numbers of new hotels that have opened. • _____ .
The economy is doing poorly these days.	• Discuss major businesses that have closed recently. • _____ .
The regional economy is changing.	• Discuss new businesses that have come to the region. • _____ .

B. Go online to watch part of the video again and write factual and statistical support for the statements listed on the left.

Oil is not the only industry in Dubai.	*Now invest in infrastructure* _____
Dubai is a center for travel and trade.	The shipping port → _____ _____ The airport → _____ _____
Dubai's free zones are good places to do business.	Taxes → _____ _____ Each free zone → _____ _____

C. Work in small groups to discuss your opinion of each statement below. What statistical and factual support could you add to strengthen your opinion?

1. All students should study abroad at least once before graduation from college.

   I disagree with this because I feel studying abroad is too expensive. So I would use statistics to show the average costs for an international student. I would also try to show employment information for students who have not studied abroad.

2. Entrance tests should not be used for university admissions.

D. As a group, present your opinion to the rest of the class. Support it with the facts and statistics you came up with in activity C.

PRONUNCIATION SKILL | Stress in Numbers

LEARN

A. See the chart below for examples of typical stress in numbers. The stressed syllable or word is in pink. Go online to listen.

Number	Stress
numbers ending in *–teen*	thir • teen
multiples of ten	thir • ty
compound numbers	for • ty • eight
hundreds	five • hun • dred
thousands	ten • thou • sand
millions	eight • mil • lion
zero	ze • ro
fractions	two • thirds

PRONUNCIATION TIPS

1. Stress the last number in a compound number: 2,458

2. The number zero can also be pronounced like the letter O, such as "Please turn to page 105 (one-oh-five)."

3. Twenty is often pronounced as "twenny."

B. In phrases, numbers may be stressed differently. See the chart below for some of these differences. The stressed syllable or word in each chunk is in pink. Go online to listen.

Number	Stress
compound numbers in hundreds and thousands (add "and")	two • hun • dred • and • two a • hun • dred • and • se • ven • ty • four
percents	eight • per • cent
numbers as adjectives	forty million passengers
years	2005 (two thousand five)

C. Shifting stress is when a word's stressed syllable changes based on how it is used in the sentence. See the chart below for examples of shifting stress in numbers ending in *–teen*. Go online to listen.

Stress on first syllable	Stress on second syllable
When counting: thirteen, fourteen, fifteen, etc.	When the number is at the end of a chunk: She's thirteen.
When numbers come before a noun: thirteen years	
To show contrast: She's thirteen, not fourteen!	

A. Go online to listen to the sentences. Notice the differences in how the numbers are stressed. Underline the stressed syllable. Repeat each sentence with appropriate stress.

1. Twenty-<u>six</u> are here.

   Twenty-six <u>per</u>cent are here.

2. There's one.

   There's one-half.

3. I see two.

   I see two hundred.

   I see two hundred people.

4. I counted forty.

   I counted fourteen.

   I counted fourteen thousand.

5. I counted fourteen pieces.

   I counted fourteen pieces, not fifteen!

6. The company has two.

   The company has two million.

   The company has two million dollars.

B. With a partner, talk about the English classes you've taken. Ask questions such as, "How many years have you studied English?" or "How many English classes have you taken?" Use appropriate stress for all numbers.

A: **How many years** have you studied English?

B: <u>Four</u>teen, on and off. **I started when I was twenty**-one. I have to use it in my job about <u>seven</u>ty-five per**cent** of the time. How many classes have you taken?

A: <u>Thir</u>teen.

End of Unit Task

Review the note-taking and presentation skills you learned in this unit. Then practice the skills as you give a presentation and listen to other presentations about cities that are good places to live and do business.

A. Work with a partner. Choose a large city that you and your partner know a lot about. Is the city a good place for doing business?

B. With your partner, list as much factual and statistical information as you can to support your opinion. Include the following factors:

• education

• health

• infrastructure

• location

• technology

• transportation

C. Develop a short presentation on whether your city is a good place to do business. Use facts and statistical support.

> *In our opinion, Dubai is a great place to do business. First, the city has a great infrastructure. Dubai also has a large international airport and shipping port. Additionally, the city has a business-friendly tax system. There are no personal or corporate income taxes. Along with this, the city has 18 economic free zones, making it easy for large international companies to trade. Finally, the city is close to two-thirds of the world's population. From Dubai, businesses are close to many people and large markets. For these reasons, we feel that Dubai is an excellent place for business.*

D. Work with another pair of students. Listen to each other's presentations.

1. As you listen, take notes using abbreviations and symbols.

2. Then using your notes, summarize the presentation that you listened to. Discuss the factual and statistical support that you heard.

3. Work with another pair of students and repeat steps 1 and 2.

Self-Assessment		
Yes	**No**	
☐	☐	I successfully used abbreviations and symbols in my notes.
☐	☐	I was able to summarize others' presentations using my notes.
☐	☐	I successfully gave a presentation.
☐	☐	I successfully used facts and statistical support in my presentation.
☐	☐	I can use stress correctly to pronounce numbers.
☐	☐	I can correctly use the target vocabulary words from the unit.

Discussion Questions

With a partner or in a small group, discuss the following questions.

1. What costs do entrepreneurs have to pay in order to start a new business?

2. What factors might a business owner consider when determining where to establish a business?

3. What is Dubai doing to attract new businesses?

UNIT 3

Enhancing Reality

In this unit, you will

> learn about augmented reality glasses and other new technologies.

> increase your understanding of the target academic words for this unit.

LISTENING AND SPEAKING SKILLS

> Signal Phrases
> Sharing Opinions Politely
> **PRONUNCIATION** Sentence Stress

Self-Assessment

Think about how well you know each target word, and check (✓) the appropriate column. I have...

TARGET WORDS	never seen this word before.	heard or seen the word but am not sure what it means.	heard or seen the word and understand what it means.	used the word confidently in *either* speaking or writing.
AWL				
currency				
detect				
🔑 devote				
duration				
🔑 exhibit				
interact				
margin				
🔑 military				
🔑 overseas				
reluctant				
🔑 substitute				
widespread				

🔑 Oxford 3000™ keywords

25

Vocabulary Activities

A. Cross out the word or phrase in parentheses with a different meaning from the others. Use a dictionary to help you understand new words. Compare answers with a partner.

1. The company's president decided to buy the augmented reality technology after he saw the large (*show* / *discussion* / *demonstration* / *exhibition*) on AR glasses.

2. Last year, he joined (*the military* / *the armed services* / *an environmental organization* / *an organization that protects and fights for the country*). He had to train with other soldiers.

3. You must first change the (*income* / *bills* / *money* / *currency*) to dollars. Then you can change your dollars to pesos. We need pesos to buy things here.

4. New computer applications allow users to (*work together with* / *look at* / *use and have an effect on* / *interact with*) virtual and computer graphics.

5. When you go (*to a foreign country* / *abroad* / *overseas* / *to another city in the same country*), you need to bring a passport with you. Sometimes you also have to pay a visa fee when you enter a new country.

6. For the (*duration* / *free time* / *the length* / *time period*) of the trip, we plan to focus on new sales. This is what we will do until the end of the trip.

Interact means "to communicate with someone." The verb *interact* is followed by the preposition *with*.

> In this class, you'll **interact with** students from different majors.

Interact can also mean "to have an effect on." People interact with things. Also, things interact with other things.

| person to thing interaction | *The touchscreen allows teachers to* **interact with** *the board as they teach.* |
| thing to thing interaction | *When the sugar* **interacted with** *the chemical, the results were surprising.* |

CORPUS

B. List examples of the different kinds of interactions shown in the chart.

Person to person interactions	Person to thing interactions	Thing to thing interactions
1. students with different majors	1. a teacher and a touchscreen	1. chemicals
2.	2.	2.
3.	3.	3.

C. *Interactive* often describes technology users can work with directly where information is passed back and forth. Match each interactive item with its purpose.

_c_ 1. An interactive menu   a. allows users to click on links in the text.

___ 2. An interactive map   b. allows users to click on products to get more information or to find store locations.

___ 3. An interactive book   c. allows users to choose their meals and get details about options.

___ 4. An interactive exhibit   d. allows users to mark locations and measure distances between different places.

___ 5. An interactive advertisement   e. allows users to touch different materials in a display to see how those materials work.

D. *Overseas* means "in a foreign country, especially those separated from your country by the ocean." Rank the importance of different reasons for taking a trip overseas. Compare your answers with a partner.

Overseas activities	Rank (1 = the most important, 6 = the least important)
Visiting historical places	
Shopping	
Seeing family or friends	
Experiencing a different culture	
Studying	
Doing outdoor activities	

E. Work with a partner. List the name of the currencies of two other countries.

1. _Japan → Yen_   3. _____

2. _USA → dollar_   4. _____

About the Topic

Virtual reality is when computer images appear to completely surround a person in a computer-created world. This differs from *augmented reality*. Augmented Reality (AR) technology combines the real world with computer information and graphics. For example, AR glasses allow users to see and use virtual graphics and computer information while at the same time seeing the real world around them.

Before You Listen

Read these questions. Discuss your answers in a small group.

1. Where do you go for road directions or information about the weather?
2. How do you use technology in your daily life?
3. What is virtual reality? Are there times when you think it is better not to use it?

Listen

Read the Listen for Main Ideas activity below. Go online to listen to Dr. Michael Adams give a lecture about how augmented reality glasses could change the way you interact with the world.

Listen for Main Ideas

Mark each sentence as *T* (true) or *F* (false). Work with a partner. Restate false sentences to make them correct.

_F_ 1. The professor discusses how the AR glasses were made.

He discusses how AR glasses work and different applications for them.

___ 2. AR glasses are useful on trips overseas.

___ 3. People trying to find jobs could use AR glasses.

___ 4. Medical students could practice surgery with AR glasses.

LISTENING SKILL | Signal Phrases

LEARN

A *signal phrase* is a group of words that tell listeners what will come next in a lecture or presentation. Paying attention to signal phrases will help follow the speaker's ideas. Look at the examples in the chart below.

Purpose	Signal phrases
Main ideas / Sequence	1. *First of all* _____
	Next, I want to talk about different applications that could work with AR glasses.
	Finally, there are some great applications for AR in health and medicine.
Examples of an idea	**For instance,** my glasses say that it's 77 degrees and sunny …
	Let's say you go on a trip overseas.
	2. _____

Additional ideas	**In addition**, AR applications can be used in education.
	Also, as you work, each group can come up ...
	3. _____
Emphasis	**Of course**, if you get bored in the library, you'll have thousands of videos and games ...
	In fact, this is something the military has already started using.
	4. _____

APPLY

Add these signal phrases beside the correct purpose in the chart above.

First of all	It's important to note that	Plus	For example

A. Read the sentences below. Then go online to listen to part of the lecture. Write the signal phrases that you hear.

1. So _____*first of all*_____, I want to show you how these AR glasses work.	Main ideas / Sequence
2. Now I'm looking out this classroom window here. With these glasses, _____ do I see everything that's outside, _____ see computer graphics with weather information.	Emphasis
3. _____, my glasses say that it's 77 degrees and sunny outside right now.	Examples of ideas
4. _____, I'm getting information on flowers and trees as I look around.	Additional ideas
5. _____, that flower over there—my glasses say that it's an azalea.	Examples
6. _____ that these glasses work as a phone, too. So I can send text messages using voice commands, and I can have a phone conversation using the glasses.	Emphasis

B. Go online to listen to another part of the lecture. Then use signal phrases from the chart above to discuss augmented reality with a partner.

1. go on a trip overseas → tour guide
2. go to a museum → information, videos related to exhibitions
3. see restaurant → menu, prices, reviews
4. exchange money → compare currency rates

Vocabulary Activities

A. The adjective *marginal* has multiple meanings. Match the dictionary definitions on the left with the example sentences on the right.

Definitions

_c_ 1. small and not important

___ 2. not part of a main group

___ 3. written in the empty space at the side of a page

Example Sentences

a. They are a marginal group that is often forgotten by the larger society.

b. The instructor wrote some marginal comments on my essay.

c. The bad weather had a marginal effect on the event. Most people still came.

B. Circle the word that is closest in meaning to the bold target word in each sentence. Underline the word that means the opposite.

1. I am **reluctant** to eat new kinds of food. I don't like to eat things that I haven't tried before.

   (unsure / certain / emotional / thoughtful)

2. The factory **substituted** robots for workers. They only use robots now.

   (replaced / made available / kept / belong)

3. The **widespread** use of smartphones has led to new computer applications.

   (unusual / interested / developed / common)

C. Fill out the chart with the amount of time you devote to each activity every week. Compare your answers with a partner.

	0–1 hour	2–5 hours	6–8 hours	9 or more hours
studying for classes				
watching TV				
meeting friends				
cleaning house				

Detect means "to discover or notice something" that is difficult to see or feel.

Humans use clues to *detect* things.

> The computer was turned on, so the manager **detected** that someone had been looking through her files.

Animals can *detect* things, too.

> Even before the ground began to shake, wild animals **detected** the earthquake and began to howl.

Many forms of technology use sensors to *detect* problems.

> A motion sensor **detected** movement outside the building and turned on bright lights.

CORPUS

D. One high-tech company recently created driverless cars with advanced detection systems. List different things that a driverless car's detection systems would need to *detect* in order to drive without human help. Discuss with a partner.

1. *other cars* _____

2. _____

3. _____

Reluctant means "hesitating before doing something because you do not want to do it or because you are not sure that it is the right thing to do." *Reluctant* is often used with the preposition *to*.

> I am **reluctant to** agree with you. I don't know if you are right about that.

CORPUS

E. Fill out the survey. Circle your answers. Discuss with a partner, using complete sentences.

1. I am reluctant to talk to people that I do not know.

agree | somewhat agree | somewhat disagree | disagree

2. I am reluctant to travel to new places. I like being in places that I know.

agree | somewhat agree | somewhat disagree | disagree

3. I am reluctant to ask for help from the teacher if I don't understand something.

agree | somewhat agree | somewhat disagree | disagree

4. I am reluctant to take risks or chances. I like to be careful.

agree | somewhat agree | somewhat disagree | disagree

About the Topic

Robot technology is developing quickly in manufacturing and medicine. Robots are increasingly doing work that is dangerous or difficult for humans. Scientists are currently debating whether it is possible for robots to think for themselves or know that they exist.

Before You Listen

Read these questions. Discuss your answers in a small group.

1. What kinds of jobs do robots do better than humans?
2. By 2050, what jobs do you think robots will do?
3. Some scientists say that robots may become self-aware in the near future. Do you think this is possible?

Listen

Read the Listen for Main Ideas activity below. Go online to listen to the discussion on new robot technology. In the discussion, Pritha Sarin and Edward Ballantyne debate the advantages and disadvantages of new robot technology in our lives.

Listen for Main Ideas

Read the questions about the listening. Work with a partner to ask and answer these questions.

1. Overall, what are Edward and Pritha's opinions on using robots?
2. What are some advantages to using robots?
3. What are some risks of people becoming dependent on robots?
4. Both Pritha and Edward think that robots becoming self-aware is unlikely. What do you think?

SPEAKING SKILL   Sharing Opinions Politely

LEARN

When you participate in academic discussions, you may *agree* or *disagree* with other people's opinions. You should be able to express your opinion with partners, small groups, or the entire class. When you disagree, do so politely.

Agreeing	Disagreeing
He's absolutely right.	I understand what you are saying, but ...
That's probably true.	I see it a little differently.
	I'm not sure that I agree.

Hedging is another way to give your opinion. When you hedge, you disagree or agree with only part of something. This shows that you respect other opinions, but you don't agree fully. When you *remain neutral*, you do not agree or disagree. You might want to hear more before you form an opinion.

Hedging	Remaining neutral
I agree with you for the most part. Except, …	I'm not sure yet.
To some extent, you are right. However, …	I'm still trying to decide what I think.
I partially agree with you, but …	

APPLY

A. Work with a partner. Answer the following questions.

1. Read the agreeing sentences on page 32. Which is the strongest? Which is the weakest?

   "He's absolutely right" is the strongest. "That's probably true" is the weakest.

2. Read the disagreeing statements on page 32. How are these sentences different from saying, "I disagree"?

3. Read the hedging statements above. What do you think is the purpose of hedging?

4. "I haven't thought about it" is not listed as a remaining neutral statement. Why might this sentence have a negative effect on a discussion?

B. Read the sentences below first. Then go online to listen to part of the audio again. Fill out the chart with sentences that the speakers use to agree, disagree, hedge, or remain neutral.

Moderator: "So, in the future, it could even become illegal for people to drive their own cars because robots will be safer drivers."	Disagreeing → Pritha: 1. _____ *Well, I see it a little differently.* _____
Pritha: "Then we stop learning, and we stop creating."	Agreeing → Edward: 2. _____
Edward: "People today spend their time doing other things, and there's nothing wrong with that."	Remaining Neutral → Moderator: 3. _____
Moderator: " … what if robots do become conscious, and start to think and be creative? Then robots really could take over almost all human roles in the workplace."	Hedging → Edward: 4. _____

C. Discuss the following question in a small group. Make sure you respond to different opinions by agreeing, disagreeing, hedging, or remaining neutral.

Overall, do you think the increasing use of robots in manufacturing is an advantage or a disadvantage?

LEARN

Words in a sentence receive different stress, often based on the word's importance to the meaning of the sentence. Content words are important for the listener to understand what the sentence is about. They are usually verbs, nouns, adjectives, adverbs, question words, and negatives. They receive the stress and are pronounced strong, long, high, and clear.

Words that are not content words, called function words, do not usually receive stress in a sentence. These words include prepositions, pronouns, conjunctions, auxiliary verbs such as *be* and *have*, and articles.

A. Go online to listen to the sentences. Notice the stressed words in pink.

1. We still need people to design and program all these new robots.

2. At the same time, I could send text messages through voice commands or have a phone conversation through my glasses.

3. What if the robot breaks down after you've become dependent on it?

APPLY

A. Go online to listen to the sentences. Fill in the missing content words.

1. I want to ___*buy*___ the ___*tablet*___ instead of the ___*phone*___.

2. _____ are the _____ _____ in this _____?

3. It is _____ that this _____ has

   _____ so _____.

4. He's _____ to his _____.

B. Go online to listen to the sentences again. Notice how the function words are not stressed and harder to hear.

C. Go online to listen to the sentences. Fill in the missing function words.

1. Substituting people ___*for*___ robots ___*in*___ ___*a*___ factory

   ___*can*___ ___*have*___ unexpected consequences.

2. _____ _____ _____ see _____ exhibit

   _____ _____ science museum.

3. _____ _____ let robots work _____ _____,

   _____ _____ _____ won't learn new things.

4. _____ military uses _____ lot _____ _____ latest equipment.

D. Go online to listen to the sentences. Underline the content words. Then say the sentences aloud. Stress the content words and unstress the function words.

1. <u>Augmented reality glasses</u> are very <u>expensive</u>.
2. I would learn so much more if I had a pair of these glasses.
3. Robots can take the place of people in some workplaces.
4. The science museum has a new interactive exhibit.
5. They are developing the new computer overseas.
6. Don't be reluctant to embrace new technology.

E. With a partner, talk about the piece of technology that you use the most. Use appropriate sentence stress in your conversation.

A: I don't **know what** I would **ever do** without my **smartphone!**

B: **What** would **happen** if you **lost** it?

End of Unit Task

Technology is an important part of our daily lives, yet people have very strong opinions about how the growth of technology affects society. Listen to a new audio in which one student expresses an opinion about technology. Practice listening for signal phrases. Then discuss your own opinions in a small group. Share opinions politely, using phrases for agreeing, disagreeing, hedging, and remaining neutral.

A. Go online to listen to a student's opinion of the growth of technology. Fill out the chart as you listen.

Purpose	Signal phrases
Main ideas / Sequence	_____*First of all*_____, I believe that the growth of technology is a major social problem among young people.
Examples	_____, studies have shown that over 60% of high school students are addicted to hi-tech devices.
Emphasis	_____, students addicted to technology exhibited loneliness and depression.
Additional ideas	_____, lack of social interaction is a problem.

B. Work with a partner. Briefly summarize the student's opinion in your own words.

C. Do you believe that the growth of technology is a good thing for society? Write some notes expressing your opinion.

Other student's notes	Your notes
A. Some think tech. good but I disagree	A. Your opinion
B. Social problem → young people	
1. 60% h.s. students addicted to tech	B. Reason and examples
2. show loneliness + depression	
C. Social interaction	C. Reason and examples
1. addiction → less interaction w/ people	
2. So, lose social skills	
D. Tech. more disadvantages than benefits	D. Restate opinion

D. Work with a partner. Discuss your opinion using your notes and the signal phrases from pages 28 and 29.

E. Work in small groups. Discuss your own and your group members' opinions. Use the expressions on pages 32 and 33 to practice agreeing, disagreeing, hedging, or remaining neutral.

Self-Assessment		
Yes	**No**	
☐	☐	I successfully identified signal phrases
☐	☐	I was able to express my opinion and respond to other students' opinions, using phrases for agreeing, disagreeing, hedging, and remaining neutral.
☐	☐	I can use proper sentence stress with content and function words.
☐	☐	I can correctly use the target vocabulary words from the unit.

Discussion Questions

With a partner or in a small group, discuss the following questions.

1. How do you think we will use augmented reality technology in the future?

2. What might be some disadvantages of augmented reality technology?

3. Do you think scientists should try to create self-aware robots? Is there value in that technology?

UNIT 4

Literary Symbols

In this unit, you will

> learn about symbolism in literature.
> increase your understanding of the target academic words for this unit.

LISTENING AND SPEAKING SKILLS

> Outlining Notes
> Giving Short Oral Summaries
> **PRONUNCIATION** Dropping the /h/ Sound

Self-Assessment

Think about how well you know each target word, and check (✓) the appropriate column. I have…

TARGET WORDS	never seen this word before.	heard or seen the word but am not sure what it means.	heard or seen the word and understand what it means.	used the word confidently in *either* speaking or writing.
AWL				
🔑 abandon				
apparent				
🔑 attitude				
🔑 category				
commence				
compatible				
🔑 context				
contradict				
🔑 labor				
overlap				
🔑 resolve				
🔑 uniform				

🔑 Oxford 3000™ keywords

Vocabulary Activities

Word Form Chart		
Noun	**Verb**	**Adjective**
category	categorize	_____
commencement	commence	_____
compatibility	_____	compatible
contradiction	contradict	contradictory
overlap	overlap	_____

A. Complete the sentences below using the correct form of the target words in the Word Form Chart. Use the words in parentheses to help you.

1. This program is _____*compatible*_____ with other computer programs. It works
   (able to be used together)

   well with any program.

2. Those two classes include a few of the same books, so there is

   some _____ between them.
   (shared area of knowledge or interest)

3. There is a _____ between the company's goal to sell overseas
   (two things not agreeing or making sense)

   and its focus on local customers only.

4. In which _____ does the book go? Does it go under history
   (group with things in common)

   or culture?

5. The meeting _____ with a speech from the president.
   (began)

6. The student _____ the professor yesterday. The student said
   (said what someone said is wrong)

   the new policy was good for people, not bad for them.

The verb *commence* is a formal word that means "to start" or "to begin."
Commence is usually not used to talk about small or everyday activities.

   X *I **commenced** reading a magazine while relaxing at home.*

   ✓ *The politician **commenced** his second term in office today.*

CORPUS

B. Write either *C* (commence) or *S* (start) in front of the activities below. Remember that *commence* is used for more formal activities.

<u>S</u> 1. dinner with friends   ____ 4. homework

____ 2. international exhibition   ____ 5. government investigation

____ 3. official meeting   ____ 6. favorite TV show

C. *Uniformity* means "the same in all parts at all times." How important is uniformity for each category? Discuss your answers with a partner.

Category	Uniformity not important	Uniformity somewhat important	Uniformity very important
1. how university students dress at school	✓		
2. the laws in different cities of a country			
3. the way a teacher grades each student in a class			
4. a company's healthcare plan for its employees			

The adjective *compatible* has different meanings:

a. able to exist together without causing problems (things)

b. able to be used together, especially machines (things)

c. having a good relationship because of similar ideas or interests (people)

The word *compatible* is often used with the preposition *with*.

> The program was not **compatible with** the computer's operating system.

CORPUS

D. Which meaning of *compatible* is used in each sentence? Match each sentence with a definition (a–c) from the box above. Compare answers with a partner.

<u>b</u> 1. Be sure to buy the memory card that is compatible with my camera.

____ 2. The sales strategy is not compatible with the company's goals.

____ 3. My roommate and I are very compatible with each other.

____ 4. I tried to download the app, but it is not compatible with my old tablet.

About the Topic

Symbols are often used in literature to represent ideas. For example, a difficult journey might represent the obstacles we face in life. Authors use symbols to help readers predict what might happen or to set the mood of a scene.

Before You Listen

Read these questions. Discuss your answers in a small group.

1. If you could recommend one book to a friend, which book would you recommend? Why?

2. What are some common symbols used in literature in your country? What do they represent?

3. Why do you think authors use symbolism in their writing?

Listen

Read the Listen for Main Ideas activity below. Go online to listen to a professor talk about a few different categories of symbols, and discuss the meanings of different symbols used in literature.

Listen for Main Ideas

Read the questions about the audio. Work with a partner to ask and answer these questions.

1. What does a rainstorm mean?

   A rainstorm often means bad news or trouble.

2. What example is given for landforms?

3. What should we consider when trying to understand what colors represent?

4. What can eagles represent?

5. What did the old clock tower represent?

NOTE-TAKING SKILL Outlining Notes

LEARN

Outlining is one way to take notes. Look at the outline of the lecture on symbols in literature on page 41. Notice how the lecture is divided into symbols and categories of symbols. Under categories of symbols, there are five sections (A–E). Then there are examples of these categories and explanations (1, 2, 3, 4 ...).

When you outline, include main ideas, supporting information, and key words. Also, do not try to write full sentences. Just write the main ideas.

Lecture Topic: Symbols in Literature

Symbols – _____ *= idea, theme, feeling*
Categories of symbols
  A. Weather
    1. rainstorm / thunder → _____

    2. rain → _____

    3. Example: Hemingway's main character walking in rain after a death

  B. _____

    1. _____ *= solving problems*

    2. e.g. in the book _____
      characters climb mountains to overcome challenges

  C. _____
    1. have different meanings

    2. meanings based on writer's _____

    3. e.g. white = wedding / _____

  D. Animals
    1. Muhammad Iqbal uses eagles in poems
    2. eagles = _____
    3. same animals, different meanings, consider _____

  E. Writer's own specific symbols

    1. _____ *= old and slow*

    2. represented town changing too slowly / _____

APPLY

A. Listen to the lecture again and fill in the outline above.

B. Compare your answers with a partner.

C. Work with a partner. Choose one of the literary symbols (A–E) from the outline above. Use the examples and explanations in the outline and your own words to summarize the category of symbols.

Vocabulary Activities

A. For the target words below, match the dictionary definitions on the left with the example sentences on the right.

attitude (noun)

Definitions

_c_ 1. the way you think or feel about something

___ 2. bodily posture, showing feeling

___ 3. confident or aggressive behavior

Example Sentences

a. The officer stood with an **attitude** of relaxation.

b. The teen had **attitude**, talking rudely to adults.

c. He has a positive **attitude** about the assignment.

labor (noun, verb)

Definitions

___ 1. all available workers in a country / company

___ 2. to try hard to do something difficult

___ 3. physical work

Example Sentences

a. The garden is the result of my **labor**.

b. The number of **laborers** in the workforce decreased.

c. They **labored** for many years, trying to save money to buy a house.

The verb *abandon* has two meanings:

a. Sometimes it means to leave someone or something behind.

　*They **abandoned** the broken motorcycle on the side of the street.*

b. *Abandon* also means "to stop supporting or helping someone; to stop believing in something."

　*They **abandoned** the project, believing it could not work.*

CORPUS

B. Which meaning of *abandon* is used in each sentence? Match each sentence with a definition (a or b) from above. Compare answers with a partner.

_a_ 1. The home was abandoned. No one had lived there for years.

___ 2. He abandoned his plan to open a restaurant after he got a new job.

___ 3. Since he wasn't listening, she abandoned her efforts to help her brother with his homework.

___ 4. The people abandoned the ship because it was sinking.

C. In what context should we understand the sentences below? Match the sentences with the correct context.

_c_ 1. historical context   a. Some East Asians think it is polite.

___ 2. cultural context   b. We have to think about profit margins.

___ 3. scientific context   c. There were no planes at that time.

___ 4. business context   d. There was not enough evidence.

D. The word *apparent* means "easy to see or understand." During your first week at college, what was apparent to you? Discuss your answers with a partner.

1. It was apparent that the classes would be hard.

    agree | somewhat agree | somewhat disagree | disagree

2. It was apparent that the students on campus studied a lot.

    agree | somewhat agree | somewhat disagree | disagree

3. It was apparent that the instructors enjoyed teaching.

    agree | somewhat agree | somewhat disagree | disagree

E. The verb *resolve* means to "find an acceptable solution to a problem or difficulty." Which problems are the hardest to resolve? Compare your answers with a partner's.

Problem	Rank each (1 = the hardest to resolve, 4 = the easiest to resolve)
a disagreement with your roommate over cleaning the kitchen	
an argument with a close friend over being late for dinner	
a problem with a noisy neighbor	
a disagreement with your instructor over the answer to a test question	

About the Topic

Jules Verne was a well-known French author in the nineteenth century. He wrote several famous books about travel and adventure. The book *Around the World in Eighty Days* was published in 1873. At the time of the book's publishing, travel was difficult, and many people didn't believe that it was possible to travel around the world in so few days.

Before You Watch

Read these questions. Discuss your answers in a small group.

1. What books have you read lately? What movies have you seen recently?
2. Many famous books have become movies. Are the movies usually as good as the books are?
3. How difficult is it to travel around the world today? What makes international travel easier today than it was in the late 1800s?

Watch

Read the Listen for Main Ideas activity below. Go online to watch a student summarize *Around the World in Eighty Days*. In the book, the main character, Phileas Fogg, claims that he can travel around the world in 80 days.

Listen for Main Ideas

Work with a partner. Discuss each sentence, and circle the correct answer based on the video.

1. Fogg decides to travel around the world because ____.

   a. he wants to prove a point   b. he wants to see the world   c. he wants to visit family

2. Fogg's trip around the world is ____.

   a. mostly easy   b. difficult   c. a failure

3. Fogg travels ____.

   a. with his friends   b. alone   c. with his assistant

4. In the end, Fogg ____.

   a. succeeds   b. arrives one week early   c. fails to finish

5. In her book report, the student says that the book teaches the reader about ____.

   a. how to travel   b. never giving up   c. competition and success

PRESENTATION SKILL   Giving Short Oral Summaries

LEARN

When you give a short oral summary, talk about main ideas and important supporting information. Also, after your summary, give your opinion or analysis of what you summarized. In the video, the student summarized *Around the World in Eighty Days* and gave her opinion of the book. She used notes to help her remember what she wanted to say. Look at the notes she used as she spoke.

Notes for Book Report:

I. Introduction	Title: Around the World in Eighty Days
	Author: Jules Verne
	Year written:
	Type of book: adventure story
	What about: Phileas Fogg + assistant travel around world
II. Body	Introduction: Fogg makes a claim → travel world 80 days
	What happens:
	1. After that, Fogg and assistant leave London
	2. Trip – many difficulties, but Fogg never gives up
	3. _____
III. Conclusion	In the end: arrive in London
	Fogg thinks he is late
	But time difference = one extra day
	_____
IV. Opinion	_____ _____ _____ _____

APPLY

A. Watch the video again. Add to the notes above. Compare your notes with a partner.

B. Prepare a short oral summary of your favorite book, movie, or TV show. Write notes (not full sentences) for yourself in a chart like the one above.

C. Using your notes, present your summary to a partner.

LEARN

A. When the /h/ sound is in the beginning of an unstressed word (such as *he, his, her,* and *him*) and follows a word with a consonant, the /h/ is often dropped.

Go online to listen to the following sentences. Notice that when the /h/ is dropped, the two words sound like one.

1. This gives him an extra day.

2. Irene is going to read her summary first.

B. Go online to listen. Notice that the /h/ sounds at the beginning of the sentences are not dropped. However, the second /h/ sounds are dropped.

1. Harper Lee used a clock tower as a symbol in her book.

2. Her decision to use the tower was her personal choice.

APPLY

A. Go online to listen. Circle the /h/ sounds that are not dropped. Draw a slash through the /h/ sounds that are dropped.

1. She used color to highlight the themes in her short story.

2. The book that he is going to recommend is his favorite.

3. She is hoping to attend her literature professor's lecture on Hemingway.

4. How does she plan to write her summary?

5. I want to thank him. He helped me understand the symbolism in the novel.

6. His book is going to get published after his agent signs the deal.

B. Say the sentences in Apply, activity A. Drop the /h/ sounds in unstressed words and link to the previous words where appropriate.

C. With a partner, talk about your favorite authors. Notice if your partner is dropping the /h/ sounds in unstressed words and linking to the previous consonant.

A: In his book *The Great Gatsby, Fitzgerald uses the color green to symbolize hope.*

B: *How does he use other colors?*

End of Unit Task

In this unit, you learned how to outline your notes and how to give short oral summaries. Review the note-taking and presentation skills by preparing a short oral summary. Use your notes as you present your summary to a small group. Then take notes on your classmates' summaries, using an outline form.

A. Think of a book you have read, or a movie or TV show you have seen recently. Fill out the chart with notes for an oral summary presentation.

I. Introduction	*The book (movie / show):*
II. Body	*In the beginning,* *After that,*
III. Conclusion	*In the end,*
IV. Opinion	*Overall,*

B. In small groups, take turns giving your oral summaries. Use your notes.

C. Listen to the other students and take notes in outline form.

I. Introduction	*Title:* *Author:* *Year written or produced:* *Type of book (movie / show):* *What it is about:*
II. Body	*Introduction:* *What happens:* *1. After that:* *2. Difficulties characters face:* *3. How they overcome the difficulties:*
III. Conclusion	*In the end:*
IV. Opinion	

Self-Assessment		
Yes	**No**	
☐	☐	I successfully prepared and gave a short oral summary.
☐	☐	I listened to a short oral summary.
☐	☐	I was able to outline my notes.
☐	☐	I can drop the /h/ sound after a consonant.
☐	☐	I can correctly use the target vocabulary words from the unit.

Discussion Questions

With a partner or in a small group, discuss the following questions.

1. What are some common symbols in stories?
2. What elements make up a good written story?
3. Do you think it is easy to write a fictional story? Why or why not?

UNIT 5

Creative Solutions

In this unit, you will

> learn about solutions for global climate change.
> increase your understanding of the target academic words for this unit.

LISTENING AND SPEAKING SKILLS

> Listening for Proposals
> Giving and Responding to Proposals
> **PRONUNCIATION** Pronouncing Nasal Sounds

Self-Assessment

Think about how well you know each target word, and check (✓) the appropriate column. I have...

TARGET WORDS	never seen this word before.	heard or seen the word but am not sure what it means.	heard or seen the word and understand what it means.	used the word confidently in *either* speaking or writing.
AWL				
🔑 domestic				
🔑 establish				
🔑 estimate				
🔑 fund				
globe				
input				
intermediate				
neutral				
🔑 output				
random				
🔑 release				
unify				

🔑 Oxford 3000™ keywords

Vocabulary Activities

Word Form Chart		
Noun	**Verb**	**Adjective**
establishment	establish	established
estimation	estimate	estimated
globe	——————	global
neutralization	neutralize	neutral
release	release	released

A. Complete the paragraph below using the correct form of the target words in the Word Form Chart.

Many scientists _____ *estimate* _____ that _____
(1. make a close calculation)   (2. worldwide)

temperatures will continue to increase. They believe that this is because

too much carbon dioxide is being _____ into the Earth's
(3. let go)

atmosphere. As a result, wind farms have been _____ in
(4. started or created)

some places. Wind farms are carbon _____, so they do not
(5. not increasing or decreasing)

change the atmosphere. However, wind farms need wind to work. If there is

no wind, wind farms do not produce electricity.

B. For the target words in bold, match each example sentence with a definition.

Definitions

_c_ 1. not supporting any side in a disagreement

___ 2. neither adding or subtracting from

___ 3. not a very bright or strong color

Example Sentences

a. New green technology may help the city become carbon **neutral**.

b. Beige is a **neutral** color.

c. When my friends argue, I try to remain **neutral**.

Definitions

___ 1. to make something available to the public

___ 2. to free someone from a duty, a responsibility, or contract

___ 3. to let something out; to stop holding something

Example Sentences

a. The company **released** a statement about its new product.

b. The company **released** water from the river.

c. The company **released** several workers this week.

C. List three things, phrases, or collocations that you can think of for each target word.

1. release a (movie / statement)   *video game, new product, greenhouse gas*

2. estimate the (amount / danger)   _____

3. neutral (color / country)   _____

D. Rank these global issues in the order of importance (1 = the most, 4 = the least). Discuss your answers with a partner.

____ Climate change

____ International hacking and Internet security

____ Poverty

____ Deforestation

E. Match the definitions of *establish* with the sentences below.

a. to start or create an organization, system, or place

b. to start a relationship or business partnership (formal)

c. to discover or prove the facts of a situation

d. to hold a position long enough to be respected

_a_ 1. A group of students established a new green technology company.

____ 2. That restaurant is well established. It has been there for 35 years.

____ 3. The technology company established a partnership with the government. The two are now working together on a new project.

____ 4. Based on research, scientists established that the Earth is warming.

____ 5. In recent years, wind farms have been established in many places.

About the Topic

Greenhouse gases, made up of carbon dioxide (CO_2), oxygen, and nitrogen, surround the Earth. Pollution thickens this layer of gases. A thicker CO_2 layer traps more of the sun's rays and makes it harder to reflect, or send back, the sun's rays into space. This increases temperatures around the Earth.

Before You Watch

Read the following questions. Discuss your answers in a small group.

1. What are some of the effects of climate change?

2. How concerned are you about climate change? Explain your answer.

3. What are some good ideas for solving climate change?

 Watch

Read the Listen for Main Ideas activity below. Go online to watch how scientists are working on technological ways to reflect the sun's rays and prevent global climate change.

Listen for Main Ideas

Work with a partner. Discuss each sentence, and circle the correct answer based on the video.

1. The carbon dioxide blanket around the Earth is _____ today than it was in the past.

   a. slightly thinner

   b. thicker

   c. much thinner

2. One solution for preventing global climate change is _____.

   a. a giant sunshade in space

   b. a new carbon blanket

   c. new nuclear technology

3. The giant sunshade would be made of _____.

   a. trillions of glass discs

   b. one large glass shade

   c. two separate discs

4. Large boats can spray seawater _____.

   a. into the carbon dioxide blanket

   b. at the sunshade

   c. into the stratocumulus clouds

5. The seawater may help _____.

   a. cool the Earth

   b. the clouds become more reflective

   c. provide energy

LEARN

A *suggestion* is an idea or plan that you mention for someone else to think about. A *proposal* is a more formal suggestion. In the video, the speaker discusses several proposals for solving climate change. She begins by discussing global climate change. Then she talks about the proposals for solving the problem and their possible results. This pattern is common when someone gives a proposal.

When you listen to a proposal. It is important to listen for:

1. The background or situation
2. The proposal
3. The desired result

APPLY

A. Go online to watch the first part of the video again. Add to the notes below for the giant sunshade proposal.

1. Background / Situation: carbon dioxide traps sun's heat and energy → Earth hotter

2. Proposal: place a giant sunshade in space
   made of trillions of glass discs

3. Result: reflect sun's rays away from Earth →

B. Go online to watch the second proposal. Add to the notes below for the seawater proposal.

1. Background / Situation: Earth getting hotter

2. Proposal: Large boats _____

3. Result: 500 liters / second every year →

C. Discuss the four proposals mentioned in the video with a partner. Of these, which proposal do you think is the best? Explain your answer.

1. Using a giant sunshade
2. Using large boats that spray seawater
3. Pumping urea into the ocean to feed the plankton that absorb carbon dioxide
4. Using synthetic trees to remove CO_2 from the air

Vocabulary Activities

A. Cross out the word or phrase in parentheses with a different meaning from the others. Compare answers with a partner. Use a dictionary as needed.

1. We have (*within the country / general / national / domestic*) programs that we use here at home and international programs that we use overseas.

2. We sent the (*funds / money / check / products*) to your bank. The total was 5,000 dollars.

3. This office is at (*a middle / a mid- / a lower / an intermediate*) level. It is between the local and central government.

4. To increase our (*production / output / amount produced / variety*) of wheat, we should buy more land.

5. The two teams (*unified / combined / divided / came together*) to create one team.

B. *Random* means done or chosen without a definite plan. Discuss with a partner. Which of these things are random? Which are not random?

the major you choose to study	the seat you choose when you come to class
the classes you take each semester	the apartment you choose to live in

The adjective *domestic* has several different meanings:

a. used in the home; connected with the home or family

b. of or inside a country; not foreign or international

c. enjoying or good at caring for a home

d. kept on farms or as pets; not wild (an animal)

CORPUS

C. Match each sentence below with the correct definition of *domestic* (a–d) from the box above. Compare your answers with a partner.

_a_ 1. The family was involved in a domestic disagreement.

____ 2. The farmer protected his domestic animals from nearby wolves.

____ 3. She enjoyed cooking and other domestic pursuits.

____ 4. That domestic law only applies to crimes committed in this country.

Word Form Chart		
Noun	**Verb**	**Adjective**
unification	unify	unified

D. Complete the paragraph below using the correct form of the target word in the Word Form Chart.

The _____unification_____ of the countries was challenging. Before the two
     (1. joining together)

countries were _____, much work had to be done. For example,
     (2. joined together)

to _____, both countries had to agree on new rules and systems.
     (3. become one)

After _____, these rules and systems were put in place by the
     (4. joining together)

new country.

E. *Input* means "time, knowledge, or ideas that you put into work or into a project to make it succeed." Think of recent tasks that you have done such as assignments, tests, projects, and presentations. Which ones would you like input on from your instructor?

1. *my presentation topic for next week* _____

2. _____

3. _____

F. Fill out the chart. Write in different outputs (what is produced) for the inputs listed below. Add one input and output of your own.

Input	Output
an ATM card	_____cash_____
seeds	_____
speakers into a computer	_____
_____	_____

About the Topic

Sometimes group work requires you to discuss different options and come to an agreement. When it comes to difficult world problems such as solving climate change, there can be a lot of good ideas to choose from but also many costs. It's important in these situations to listen carefully and think critically.

Before You Listen

Read these questions. Discuss your answers in a small group.

1. What are some ways to conserve energy at home, at work, and in school?

2. What is a good environmental conservation program in your country? Describe what makes the program effective.

3. What do you think is the best way to prevent climate change?

Listen

Read the Listen for Main Ideas activity below. Go online to listen to three students in a study session. They are preparing to present a proposal for solving climate change. Listen to the interaction between the students discussing their proposals.

Listen for Main Ideas

Mark each sentence as *T* (true) or *F* (false). Work with a partner. Restate false sentences to make them correct.

_F_ 1. Increased CO_2 is making the Earth colder. *It's making it hotter.*

___ 2. One proposal is to use government funds to develop new technology.

___ 3. Sometimes new technology is developed too quickly.

___ 4. One proposal is to tax companies that release carbon.

SPEAKING SKILL | Giving and Responding to Proposals

LEARN

Use *must* or *have to* to make a proposal sound stronger. However, using a softer tone can also be effective. For example, if you are suggesting an idea to your instructor or boss, a softer tone is usually better.

Standard tone	Stronger tone	Softer tone
We should use …	**We must** use …	You could use …
My suggestion is to use	She has to use …	She might want to use …
I recommend using …	You have no choice but to use …	**Maybe we could** use …

Consider how these sentences differ.

a. We must use her idea to solve this problem.

b. We might want to use her idea to solve this problem.

Responding to Suggestions

Before you express concerns or criticism, give positive feedback. This will establish a positive tone, and the person you are talking to will be more open to listening to what you say.

Positive feedback	Concern / Criticism
That's a good idea.	I'm not sure if an energy conservation program would really be enough.
I like that suggestion.	I guess my only worry would be time.
That's a great point.	The only issue I see is that companies might lose so much money on taxes that workers could lose their jobs.
That would be interesting.	It might be difficult to present all three ideas.

Consider how these responses differ.

a. I just don't think that your idea would work. Let's do something else.

b. That is a creative idea, but I am a little worried about whether it can work.

APPLY

A. Go online and listen to the discussion again. Take notes on the three proposals and the responses that follow.

Proposal	Positive response	Concern / Criticism
Developing an energy conservation program	That's a good idea.	I am not sure if an energy conservation program *would really be enough*_____ .
Using government funds to develop technology	I like _____ _____ .	I guess my only worry would be time.
Taxing companies that _____ _____	That's a great point.	The only issue I see is that companies might lose so much money on taxes that workers could lose their jobs.

B. Work with a partner. Choose the proposal that you like best. Discuss three different ways to give the same proposal.

1. standard tone   2. stronger tone   3. softer tone

C. Work in a small group with classmates who each chose different proposals. Discuss the three proposals. Give positive feedback and express one concern about each. Which is the best of the three proposals? Why?

LEARN

Nasal sounds include the sounds made by the letters *m, n,* and *ng.* They are called *nasal* because air flows through the nose to create the sound. Say the following three words out loud and listen to the difference in the sounds: *sun, sum,* and *sung.*

A. The /m/ sound is pronounced by pressing the lips together when the mouth is closed. Go online to listen to the examples of the /m/ sound.

from	random	temperature	time

B. The /n/ sound is pronounced by opening the mouth and pressing the tip of the tongue to the roof of the mouth just behind the upper teeth. Go online to listen to the examples of the /n/ sound. Then say the words yourself.

carbon	conservation	input	intermediate

C. The /ŋ/ sound is pronounced by raising the back part of the tongue to the back of the top of the mouth. It is important that the mouth is open. Go online to listen to the examples of the final /ŋ/ sound.

long	reducing	releasing	warming

APPLY

A. Go online to listen to the audio selection. Circle the word that you hear.

1. (bam)	ban	bang	4. king	Kim	kin
2. din	ding	dim	5. ran	rang	ram
3. whim	wing	win	6. sim	sin	sing

B. Practice the words in Apply, activity A. Say all the words out loud.

C. In the following sentences, underline the nasal sounds. Then say the sentences with a partner.

1. I'm always hearing about random ideas.

2. That's definitely an approach that we need.

3. By implementing the program, we could cut down on energy use.

4. We know that our energy consumption is contributing to climate change.

5. Even if we learn to conserve more of our resources, the world's population is projected to reach eight billion people within the next few years.

6. What about taking a comprehensive approach and recommending all three for our presentation?

D. **With a partner, discuss how you conserve energy. Use words with nasal sounds.**

> A: I plan on reducing my energy use by unplugging my electronics when I remember to.
>
> B: I intend on doing this all the time!

<table>
<tr><td>**PRONUNCIATION TIP**</td></tr>
<tr><td>Close your mouth for *m*.</td></tr>
<tr><td>Keep your mouth open for *n*.</td></tr>
<tr><td>Keep your mouth open for *ng*.</td></tr>
<tr><td>Tongue tip up for *n*.</td></tr>
<tr><td>Tongue tip down for *ng*.</td></tr>
</table>

End of Unit Task

In this unit, you learned how to listen for proposals. You also learned about giving your own proposals and how to respond to other students' proposals. Review these skills by discussing proposals for an issue, a challenge, or a problem on campus. Listen to other proposals, give positive feedback, and offer criticism.

A. **Work with a partner.**

1. Think of three issues, challenges, or problems on campus.

2. Choose one issue and discuss your proposals for solving the problem. Use the language in the box on page 56.

3. Choose one of your proposals. Outline your proposal for resolving a problem on campus.

Situation	
Proposal	
Result	

B. Work in a small group.

1. Listen to and take notes on your classmates' proposals.

Situation	
Proposal	
Result	

2. Give positive feedback and one concern or criticism for one or more of the proposals you listened to.

Self-Assessment		
Yes	**No**	
☐	☐	I successfully discussed different proposals.
☐	☐	I successfully outlined a proposal for resolving a problem.
☐	☐	I successfully gave my proposal.
☐	☐	I took notes and responded to other students' proposals.
☐	☐	I was able to give positive feedback and one criticism.
☐	☐	I can pronounce final nasal sounds.
☐	☐	I can correctly use the target vocabulary words from the unit.

Discussion Questions

With a partner or in a small group, discuss the following questions.

1. What are the causes of climate change?
2. What are some possible solutions to climate change?
3. Do you believe governments should take action to prevent climate change?

UNIT

6

What to Eat

In this unit, you will

> learn about recent studies on nutrition.
> increase your understanding of the target academic words for this unit.

LISTENING AND SPEAKING SKILLS

> The Cornell Method to Take Notes
> Preparing Well-Organized Presentations
> PRONUNCIATION Dropping Syllables

Self-Assessment

Think about how well you know each target word, and check (✓) the appropriate column. I have…

TARGET WORDS	never seen this word before.	heard or seen the word but am not sure what it means.	heard or seen the word and understand what it means.	used the word confidently in *either* speaking or writing.
AWL				
🔑 chemical				
comprehensive				
consume				
🔑 mental				
portion				
🔑 priority				
rigid				
supplement				
🔑 survey				
🔑 target				
tense				
🔑 visible				

 Oxford 3000™ keywords

Vocabulary Activities

Word Form Chart			
Noun	**Verb**	**Adjective**	**Adverb**
_____	_____	comprehensive	comprehensively
consumer consumption	consume	consumed	_____
supplement	supplement	supplementary	_____
target	target	targeted	_____

A. Complete the paragraph below using the correct form of the target words in the Word Form Chart.

Last year, researchers did a _comprehensive_ study. The _____
                (1. complete)   (2. point of focus)

group for the study was college students. In particular, the study looked

at most college students' _____ of "super foods," such as leafy
                    (3. eating)

green vegetables and berries. The study found that most college students

do not _____ enough leafy green vegetables. The study also said
      (4. eat)

that students who do not eat enough vegetables might want to take a

vitamin _____ .
(5. a thing that is added for improvement)

B. The noun *target* has multiple meanings. Match the dictionary definitions on the left with the example sentences on the right.

Definitions

_c_ 1. to aim an attack or a criticism at someone or something

___ 2. a result that you are trying to achieve

___ 3. a point or an area of focus

___ 4. an object that people shoot at

Example Sentences

a. The salesperson's target neighborhood was Soho.

b. We need to reach our sales target by the end of the month.

c. He was the target of their jokes.

d. He pointed his bow and arrow at the target.

The word *chemical* can refer to both natural and unnatural substances. *Artificial chemicals* are unnatural chemicals that have been created or changed by people; they did not happen naturally.

*Saccharine is an **artificial chemical** that is used as a substitute for sugar.*

CORPUS

C. Fill out the chart on chemicals. Compare your answers with a partner.

Food	Contains many artificial chemicals	Contains some artificial chemicals	Contains only natural chemicals	Not sure
chewing gum	✓			
soda				
milk				
organic blueberries				

D. Write the letter of the correct meaning of *consume* in front of each sentence.

a. to use time, fuel, or energy   c. to completely destroy something

b. to eat or drink something   d. to fill someone with a strong feeling

_b_ 1. A lot of people consume foods high in fat. However, some fatty foods are difficult for our bodies to process or digest.

___ 2. He consumes a small portion of fish once a week.

___ 3. The fire quickly consumed the wood.

___ 4. The audience was consumed by the speaker's powerful voice and message.

___ 5. New green technology helps homes consume less electricity.

E. The word *comprehensive* means "including all, or almost all, the items, details, facts, or information." Look at the pair of phrases for each problem below. Circle the phrase that is most likely to be comprehensive.

1. a. a history class that discusses two time periods in your country's history
   b. a history class that discusses the entire history of your country

2. a. a nutrition plan for all your meals and snacks
   b. a nutrition plan for one day of the week

3. a. a book that talks about all aspects of nutrition and health
   b. a book that talks about a few fruits and vegetables

About the Topic

Nutrition is a part of every person's life because it is the way that the body gets what it needs from food. Everyone must take responsibility for his or her own food choices. Unfortunately, making choices about the foods we eat can be difficult.

Before You Listen

Read these questions. Discuss your answers in a small group.

1. Where is the best place on or near campus to get a healthy meal? What makes the food there healthier than other choices?

2. Is good nutrition usually the same for everyone, or do people often have unique or special nutritional needs? What are your nutritional needs?

3. What is the best way to maintain a healthy diet?

Listen

Read the Listen for Main Ideas activity below. Go online to listen to Dr. Eric Craft lecture on the future of nutrition. His class reviews recent research in nutrition and how health experts plan to help people develop their own unique, or special, nutrition plans.

Listen for Main Ideas

Mark each sentence as *T* (true) or *F* (false). Work with a partner. Restate false sentences to make them correct.

_T_ 1. The information from different health studies can be confusing.

____ 2. In the past, nutrition plans were for individual people.

____ 3. Good nutrition is the same for all people.

____ 4. Family history may affect your nutritional needs.

____ 5. In the future, the challenge is to find a single nutrition plan for everyone.

NOTE-TAKING SKILL   The Cornell Method to Take Notes

LEARN

To take notes using the Cornell Method, divide your paper into three sections:

- Section B: Write notes in class.
- Section A: Form questions like those you might find on an exam.
- Section C: Summarize what you heard.

These three sections will help you take effective notes, study what you wrote down, and remember what you heard. Look at the notes on page 65, and read the instructions beside each section.

Section A	Section B
· What kinds of nutrition plans did experts make in the past?	· In past – experts studied food; made comprehensive plans
· Why do people have different nutritional needs?	· Food and food chemicals = different effects on different people
	· New research = individual needs
	· People are unique
· _____ _____	· Examples: 1. height, weight
	2. age
	3. _____
· _____	Nutrition Target = _____
_____	In future = _____

1. Take notes here. Compare your notes with a partner. Then add information.

2. Write questions here about the notes you took in Section B.

3. Here, write a summary of the notes from Section B.

Section C

APPLY

A. Listen to the audio again and complete Section B in the chart above.

B. Compare your answers with a partner. Then add any additional information that you remember from the lecture.

C. Write a question in Section A for each point in Section B. Work with a partner. Ask and answer each other's questions. Confirm or correct the information in Section B.

D. As a class, write a summary of the lecture in Section C.

Vocabulary Activities

Word Form Chart		
Noun	**Adjective**	**Adverb**
mentality	mental	mentally
tension	tense	tensely
rigidity	rigid	rigidly
visibility	visible	visibly

A. Complete the paragraph below using the correct form of the target words in the Word Form Chart.

Last year, I went to see my doctor to discuss my diet. I knew I was

overweight. As I explained my daily eating habits, the doctor was

___visibly___ surprised. I started to feel _____ as he explained
(1. clearly)   (2. worried and nervous)

to me that I needed to change my diet immediately. Since then, my

_____ toward nutrition has changed. I have a much healthier diet,
(3. attitude)

and I follow a _____ exercise plan that I must do every day for one
(4. strict)

hour. Nowadays, my friends say that I look _____ healthier. I can
(5. noticeably)

also say that my _____ focus has improved significantly.
(6. connected to the mind)

The verb *survey* means "to investigate the opinions or behavior of a group of people by asking them a series of questions."

> We **surveyed** the students about their favorite classes.

Survey also means "to study and give a general description of" or "to look carefully at the whole of" something.

> His book **surveyed** the history of World War II.

> The manager **surveyed** the building for damage.

CORPUS

B. Write the letter of the correct definition of *survey* next to each sentence.

a. to look carefully at something

b. to study and give a general description of something

c. to investigate the opinion of people by asking them questions

_c_ 1. The tourism students surveyed travelers to find out what they liked.

___ 2. The worker surveyed the construction site for possible dangers.

___ 3. In this course, we will survey the history of India.

___ 4. The people were surveyed on their health habits. They were asked 10 questions.

___ 5. We surveyed the damage caused by a recent tornado.

C. *Rigid* means "strict and difficult to change" and often refers to rules or methods. How rigid are the following activities for you?

Activities	Extremely rigid	Somewhat rigid	Not rigid
Your exercise routine			✓
Your diet			
Your parents' rules for you in high school			
The graduation requirements for your major			

D. A *portion* is an appropriate amount of food for one person. What is your diet like?

1. I often eat a large portion of _____ .

2. I often eat a small portion of _____ .

3. My favorite restaurant serves (large / small / average) portions.

E. The word *priority* refers to "something that you think is more important than other things." Rank each activity in the chart below (1 = the highest priority, 4 = the lowest priority).

Your priorities for this class	Rank
Memorizing vocabulary words and other phrases	
Knowing different grammar tenses	
Being able to write clearly	
Having good pronunciation	

About the Topic

Research has shown that food impacts much more than a person's body. Some nutrients can put a person in a better mood. Others help with concentration and memory. More and more, people are choosing healthy foods not only to look their best but also to feel their best.

Before You Listen

Read these questions. Discuss your answers in a small group.

1. What foods help to prevent sickness? Do you eat these foods regularly?

2. Which foods increase your energy?

3. Is it expensive to have a healthy diet? Are unhealthy foods cheaper than healthier foods?

Listen

Read the Listen for Main Ideas activity below. Go online to listen to a presentation on nutrition for university students. University student Tiffany Bradford talks about foods that can increase brainpower, increase energy, and prevent sickness.

Listen for Main Ideas

Read the questions about the presentation. Work with a partner to ask and answer these questions.

1. Why is the number 60 important?

   Sixty percent of all students surveyed did not understand the positive effects of food on their bodies and minds.

2. What foods help increase brainpower?

3. Why are leafy green vegetables good?

4. Why is yogurt mentioned?

5. What does the student say about a healthier diet and money?

PRESENTATION SKILL Preparing Well-Organized Presentations

LEARN

As a student, you may be asked to give a formal presentation. Organizing your presentation into different parts and using clear language is very important. A well-organized presentation has three sections: an introduction, a body, and a conclusion. Look at the left column of the chart on page 69 to see the different points that you can include in each section. Look at the language in the right column that will help your audience understand your presentation.

I. Introduction 1. Greet your audience. Say what your topic is. 2. Tell your audience how many points you will make.	**Examples** **Good afternoon. Today, I will be discussing** ways to use food to improve your body and mind. **So, I'm going to talk about** three important kinds of foods: food to increase brainpower, _____*food to increase energy*_____ , and _____ .
II. Body 1. Introduce each point using clear signal phrases as you move from point to point. 2. Give examples and supporting information under each point. Use facts, statistics, quotations, specific examples, etc.	**So** _____ with food for increasing brainpower. oily fish, e.g. salmon / mackerel, have omega 3 omega 3 → improve memory / concentration soy, e.g. tofu / miso soup, support _____ _____ , I am going to talk about food you can eat to increase your energy. leafy green vegetables, e.g. kale → vitamins / minerals apples – fiber → prevent sleepiness water → energy _____ , let's highlight some great foods for improving your ability to prevent sickness. yogurt – healthy bacteria fights diseases vitamin C, e.g. bell peppers and oranges ↓ colds by 30% or more
III. Conclusion 1. Summarize your main points. 2. Thank your audience and take questions.	**To summarize**, today we've talked about improving _____ , increasing _____ , <u>and preventing</u> _____ . Thank you very much. Any questions?

APPLY

A. Go online to listen to the first part of the presentation. As you listen, fill in the blanks and add to the notes in the Introduction above.

B. Go online to listen to the rest of the presentation. Fill in the blanks and add to the notes above. Compare your notes with a partner.

C. Work in a small group and create a short presentation on how to have a healthy diet. Use the ideas in the left column of the chart above to prepare your own presentation. Each member of your group should do a different part of the presentation.

D. Share your presentation with another group.

PRONUNCIATION SKILL Dropping Syllables

LEARN

Words with more than one syllable can sometimes lose a syllable when spoken.

In some words, you drop, or reduce, the vowel sound in the unstressed syllable.

 A. Go online to listen to the words below. You delete vowel sounds when you say these words.

Word	Deleted vowel sound	Sounds like ...
chocolate	chocølate	cho • clate
different	diffǿrent	diff • rcnt
every	evǿry	ev • ry

 B. Go online to listen to the next group of words. When the speaker is talking quickly, you won't hear all the syllables.

Word	Deleted vowel sound	Sounds like ...
family	famíly	fam • ly
garage	gárage	grage
police	pólice	pleece
suppose	súppose	spose

APPLY

 A. Go online to listen to the words with dropped syllables. Cross out the deleted syllable.

1. cam • er • a
2. soph • o • more
3. com • for • ta • ble
4. fa • vor • ite
5. res • taur • ant
6. ve • ge • ta • ble

 B. Go online to listen to the words. Write the number of syllables you hear.

Word	Number of syllables heard	Word	Number of syllables heard
1. beverage	2	4. interesting	
2. several		5. extraordinary	
3. broccoli		6. generally	

C. Say the words in Learn, activities A and B. Delete the vowel sound of the dropped syllables.

D. With a partner, talk about the foods you eat. Use the words from the word bank. Delete the vowel sound of the dropped syllables.

> A: My fam~i~ly and I try to eat fruit ev~e~ry day.
>
> B: I do, too. But I like to try diff~e~rent foods on the weekends. My fav~o~rite rest~au~rant serves Ethiopian food.

every	family
chocolate	different
favorite	restaurant
comfortable	suppose

End of Unit Task

To practice what you've learned in this unit, prepare a presentation in a small group. Then listen to other presentations and take notes using the Cornell Method.

A. Work in groups of three. Use the chart on page 69 to prepare a presentation on one of the following topics.

1. a great place to travel or study abroad
2. a healthy diet or nutritional plan to follow
3. a good career to have

B. Assign each of the three parts (introduction, body, conclusion) of the presentation to each student in your group.

C. Take turns sharing your presentation with another group.

D. As you listen to the other group, take notes using the Cornell Method.

Section A	Section B
Section C	

E. With your group, create study questions about the information you wrote in Section B. Write these questions in Section A.

F. With your group, create a summary of your notes and write it in Section C.

G. Share your summary with the group whose presentation you listened to. Check that you have summarized each other's presentations correctly.

		Self-Assessment
Yes	**No**	
☐	☐	I successfully prepared a presentation.
☐	☐	I successfully gave one part of a presentation to another group.
☐	☐	I successfully took notes using the Cornell Method.
☐	☐	I wrote three questions in my notes about the presentation that I listened to.
☐	☐	I was able to write a summary of the presentation that I listened to.
☐	☐	I can correctly identify and pronounce words with dropped syllables.
☐	☐	I can correctly use the target vocabulary words from the unit.

Discussion Questions

With a partner or in small group, discuss the following questions.

1. What are examples of healthy foods? Why is each type of food considered "good for you"?

2. Do you think eating vegetables makes a significant difference in your health?

3. Why do you think people eat junk food even though they know it's not healthy?

UNIT 7

Working in the Field

In this unit, you will
> learn about careers in geology.
> increase your understanding of the target academic words for this unit.

LISTENING AND SPEAKING SKILLS
> Listening for Implications
> Polite Requests and Interruptions
> **PRONUNCIATION** Three-Word Phrasal Verbs

Self-Assessment
Think about how well you know each target word, and check (✓) the appropriate column. I have…

TARGET WORDS	never seen this word before.	heard or seen the word but am not sure what it means.	heard or seen the word and understand what it means.	used the word confidently in *either* speaking or writing.
AWL				
🔑 alter				
🔑 approximate				
🔑 aspect				
🔑 credit				
insert				
motive				
ongoing				
outcome				
🔑 restrict				
scenario				
🔑 seek				
🔑 shift				

🔑 Oxford 3000™ keywords

Vocabulary Activities

Word Form Chart		
Noun	**Verb**	**Adjective**
alteration	alter	alterable alternate
restriction	restrict	restricted
motivation motive	motivate	motivated

A. Complete the paragraph below using the correct form of the target words in the Word Form Chart.

Last week, my boss finally ___*altered*___ my work schedule. I had been
(1. made different)

working late at night. Because I was working the night shift, I did not see my

family very often. When my children were home from school, I was at work,

so I was really _____ in what I could do with them. However, now
(2. limited)

that I am working during the day, those _____ are gone. I am also
(3. limitations)

much happier and more _____ at work.
(4. interested and enthusiastic)

B. *Seek* is often used in more formal situations. The past form of *seek* is *sought*.
Write the letter of the meaning of *seek* used in each sentence.

a. to try to obtain or achieve something	b. to look for something or someone

___*a*___ 1. We are seeking funding for the new children's hospital. We are thankful
for your help.

_____ 2. The animal researchers sought the Siberian tiger in the national park but
never found it.

_____ 3. The company is seeking new areas to explore. They have been looking
into producing different products.

_____ 4. I wrote, "Seeking Employment in the Geology Industry" on my resume.
I really want to work as a geologist.

C. A *scenario* is "a description of how things might happen in the future." Here, the word *case* means event or situation. Choose the phrase from the box that best describes each situation.

the worst-case scenario	the best-case scenario
a real-life scenario	an unrealistic scenario

1. If we have to close the business, the workers would lose their jobs.

   That would be _the worst-case scenario_____.

2. If we could show events as they really occur, we could create

   _____.

3. If we won all of the games and the championship that would be

   _____.

4. The plan does not consider real situations. You have created

   _____.

The word *shift* has several different meanings:

1. to move from one position or place to another

   *He **shifted** the chairs to make more space.*

2. to change your opinion or attitude; to change the way you do something

   *The professor **shifted** the focus of the class from history to politics.*

3. to change gears when you are driving a vehicle

   *When he **shifted** gears, the bus made a strange sound.*

4. a period of time worked by a group of workers

   *He needs extra money, so he has been working the night **shift**.*

CORPUS

D. Work with a partner. What other words or phrases can you add to the chart?

Things you might shift from one position to another	Ways of thinking that can shift	Modes of transportation with gear shifts	Work shifts
1. _a chair_____	1. _class focus___	1. _a bus_____	1. _night shift____
2. _____	2. _____	2. _____	2. _____
3. _____	3. _____	3. _____	3. _____

About the Topic

Extreme heat and pressure continue to shape the Earth every day. Geology is the study of how natural features like mountains, caves, and the ocean floor are constantly changing. These changes can benefit humans by creating useful minerals like iron or can harm humans through disasters like earthquakes.

Before You Listen

Read these questions. Discuss your answers in a small group.

1. Would you prefer to work outside or in an office? If a job paid well, would you work in a remote place?

2. Geology is the study of the structure and composition of the Earth. What do you think geologists do?

3. What are the three most important aspects of a good job (income, vacation time, work hours, coworkers, or something else)?

Listen

Read the Listen for Main Ideas activity below. Go online to listen to the show *Career Exhibit*. In this episode, an environmental geologist, an exploration geologist, and an engineering geologist explain what they do.

Listen for Main Ideas

Mark each sentence as *T* (true) or *F* (false). Work with a partner. Restate false sentences to make them correct.

_T_ 1. Geologists work outside and in offices.

___ 2. An environmental geologist tries to find oil and gas.

___ 3. Exploration geologists sometimes work in remote locations.

___ 4. Engineering geologists try to save as many trees in a community as possible.

___ 5. Jobs for geologists don't pay well.

LISTENING SKILL   Listening for Implications

LEARN

Recognizing *implications* will help you understand what a speaker is saying. When a speaker *implies* something, he suggests it without actually saying it. The message is not stated directly.

For example, suppose that you own a car, and a friend tells you, "I have to go back to my hometown tomorrow for a family event. The bus ride is almost five hours long. I'm afraid I'll miss the event! Driving there would be so much faster. I wish I had a car."

His statement can have two meanings:

The meaning that is stated: The bus ride to my hometown is so long that I might miss an important family event. It would be better if I had a car.

The meaning that is implied: Can I borrow your car?

He has not asked directly to borrow your car, but because he mentions that the trip will be too long without a car, the question is *implied*.

APPLY

A. Go online to listen to the first part of the audio. What is implied, or what can you infer, about the following sentences?

1. "The short answer is that geology is the study of the structure or composition of the Earth."

    a. Geology is much more complex than the sentence explains.

    b. The definition of geology is easy to understand.

2. "So geologists almost never find themselves sitting at the same desk and doing the same thing every day."

    a. Jobs that require you to stay in one place and repeat tasks are boring.

    b. Jobs that require an understanding of both nature and management are too difficult.

B. Read the statements below. Then go online to listen to the last part of the audio. Complete the chart.

Statement	Notes	Implication
"And it's a good thing that I have my love of nature to motivate me."	– Work in remote areas for weeks *sleep in a tent* – Worked in cold for months – _____ twelve different places	The work itself is not always motivating.
"Sometimes architects have had to alter their plans based on my recommendations, and it's turned out to be very lucky that they did."	– Look at rocks, soil, _____, above and below ground – Looking for possible landslides, water leaks, _____	_____ _____ _____ _____

C. Work with a partner. Discuss the implication, or inference, you wrote for the second statement.

SPEAKING

Vocabulary Activities

A. Cross out the word or phrase in parentheses with a different meaning from the other choices. Use a dictionary to help you understand new words. Compare answers with a partner.

1. He went to the bank to find out how much (*credit / borrowed money / money to be repaid in the future / ~~foreign currency~~*) he could get for his new business.

2. Finding (*someone to borrow money from / a creditor / a bank that gives loans / someone who receives a loan*) can be difficult for new businesses.

3. The (*cause / result / outcome / effect*) of his visit to the bank was quite positive.

4. The bank gave him a loan of (*approximately / around / about / exactly*) $30,000.

5. Because of the loan, his (*ongoing / continuing / difficult / constant*) problem with money has been solved for the moment.

B. The word *credit* has multiple meanings. Match the dictionary definitions on the left with the example sentences on the right.

Definitions

_a_ 1. praise or approval for a good act

___ 2. arrangement to pay later for something you buy now

___ 3. money that you borrow from a bank; a loan

___ 4. a unit of study successfully completed at a college or school

Example Sentences

a. The researchers received a lot of credit for their hard work.

b. The student got two credits for completing the course.

c. The geologist bought the equipment he needed on credit.

d. The company was doing badly, so the bank wouldn't give them credit.

C. *Ongoing* means "continuing to exist or develop." Circle the items that are ongoing. Explain your answers to a partner.

1. (this semester) / your time in high school / last week's lecture / a movie you saw recently

2. a building that will be built next year / a building that is currently being built

3. a school project that you are working on at the moment / a school project you will start to work on later

The word *insert* means "to put something into something else." It can also mean "to add something to a piece of writing."

*I **inserted** my bank card into the ATM.*

*She **inserted** a new sentence into the email to make the meaning clearer.*

CORPUS

D. Write sentences to answer the following questions using a form of the verb *insert*.

1. How do you unlock the door to your home?

   I insert my key in the lock and turn it to unlock the door.

2. What can you insert into your cellphone when you need to charge the battery?

   _____

3. What can you add to the end of an essay to remind your readers of your main ideas?

   _____

4. If a sentence is missing an action word, what can you add to the sentence?

   _____

E. The word *aspect* is "a particular part or feature of a situation, an idea, or a problem." Fill in the blanks with a word or phrase that fits the question. Take turns asking and answering the questions with a partner.

1. What aspects of _____*your major*_____ do you enjoy?

2. What aspects of _____ do you dislike?

3. What aspects of _____ are unique or special?

4. What aspects of _____ were successful?

5. What aspects of _____ do you need to study more?

F. The adverb *approximately* is used to show that something is almost correct but not completely. Circle the word that best matches *approximately* in the sentences below.

1. The train trip takes ((about) / *exactly*) three hours.
2. You will be paid (*around* / *only*) $10 an hour.
3. There will be (*close to* / *just*) 50 people at the study session.
4. The price is (*certainly* / *nearly*) $1,000.

About the Topic

New, cheaper methods for removing unwanted chemicals, bacteria, and viruses from water are becoming available around the world. It is easier to purify water at home than most people think. You can build a system yourself with a few items you probably have in your house right now.

Before You Watch

Read these questions. Discuss your answers in a small group.

1. Do you enjoy being outdoors? What activities do you like to do outdoors?

2. What skills are useful to know when a person is in a remote location?

3. Is it safe to drink water from a river or stream? Why or why not?

Watch

Read the Listen for Main Ideas activity below. Go online to watch an interview with a geologist who explains how to make a biosand water filter. He also shares how these water filters are being used to help people around the world.

Listen for Main Ideas

Read the questions about the video. Work with a partner to ask and answer these questions.

1. Where does the geologist work? *He works outdoors in remote areas.*

2. What are the three layers of a biosand water filter?

3. What removes bad smells and tastes from the water?

4. Does the biosand water filter remove all bacteria and viruses from the water?

5. How can this type of water filter help people?

SPEAKING SKILL Polite Requests and Interruptions

LEARN

A *polite request* is the action of asking for something formally. Being able to make polite requests is important in academic and professional settings.

Polite requests
Would you explain more about the filter?
Could you explain more about the filter?
If you have time, could you explain more about the filter?
Would it be possible to explain more about the filter?

When you interrupt people, you start speaking before they have completely finished. Interrupting is a difficult skill because you need to stop the speaker at the appropriate time and in a polite way.

When you might consider interrupting ...		When you might avoid interrupting ...
group discussion	study session	class presentation
class discussion	discussion with a partner	professor's lecture

Polite ways to interrupt
If I could just stop you for a moment, *what is the purpose of the sand?*
I'm sorry to interrupt, but *where did you learn how to do this?*
I'd like to clarify: *this system cleans most bacteria?*
Would you mind if I commented on *that point?*

APPLY

A. **Work with a partner. Discuss different polite requests for the situations below.**

1. You want to discuss your homework assignment with your professor.

2. You want the instructor to explain what has just been said again.

3. Before the presenter leaves, you want to know more about where biosand filters are used.

B. **Read the statements below. Then watch the video again and fill in the blanks.**

Host: He's going to explain how a biosand water filter works.

Geologist: Wet sand goes on top of that. This sand layer should be thicker than the stone layers.

Geologist: The sand ... acts as a filter to remove bad smells and tastes from the water and, most importantly, can eliminate many viruses and bacteria from the water.

Geologist: Now a little tube gets inserted on the side ... the dirty water will filter through ...

Geologist: It can reduce turbidity as well as the percentage of pathogens, like bacteria and viruses and ...

1. Host: First of all, _could you explain_ how you learned to make a water filtration system?

2. Host: Now _____ just stop you for a moment ...

3. Host: _____ sand do you have to use?

4. Host: _____, could you tell us if biosand filters will completely purify the water?

5. Host: I'd _____—it won't produce *perfectly* clean water.

LEARN

A phrasal verb is a two- or three-word phrase with a verb followed by a word that looks like a preposition. It means something different than what the verb means by itself.

A. Go online to listen to the three-word phrasal verbs and their meanings.

Three-word phrasal verb	Meaning	Three-word phrasal verb	Meaning
cut down on	reduce	give up on	stop doing something
check up on	examine	keep up with	follow, be informed about
drop out of	not be a part of anymore	look forward to	be excited about
fall back on	rely on another idea	think back on	think about or reflect on

B. The second word in a three-word phrasal verb is stressed. Link consonant and vowel sounds when possible. Go online to listen.

He had to <u>drop **out** of</u> science club when he got a part-time job.

I <u>keep **up** with</u> the group's progress by reading their blog.

APPLY

A. Go online to listen to the sentences. Fill in the missing three-word phrasal verbs that you hear.

1. Please _____*check up on*_____ the latest results from the experiment.

2. If they want us to restrict our spending, we have to _____ costs.

3. I'm _____ hearing the outcome of the study.

4. _____ all the people who helped with the study so that you can give them credit.

5. I was just about to _____ the project when we got the outcome we were hoping for.

6. Geologists have to _____ the latest research.

7. If I don't get the job abroad, I can always _____ a position closer to home.

8. He might have to _____ graduate school if he doesn't get a scholarship.

B. Say the phrasal verbs in Learn, activity A. Stress the second word in each, and link consonant and vowel sounds when possible.

C. With a partner, use the phrasal verbs from the chart to ask each other questions. Remember to stress the second word in each and to link the consonant and vowel sounds when possible.

> A: Are you looking **forward** to your vacation home?
>
> B: I am. Do you still keep **up** with your old friends?
>
> A: I do, and we talk about fun things that we've done. Do you ever think **back** on your childhood and the friends you had then?

End of Unit Task

In this unit you learned how to listen for inferences. You also learned how to make polite requests and to interrupt politely. Review these skills by discussing a memorable experience. As you review, use inferences, polite requests, and polite interruptions.

A. Think of a memorable event or experience in your life (a trip, a big decision, a mistake, an achievement, a funny situation). Use the chart below to write a brief summary of your experience.

I. Introduction	Memorable Experience: What: When:
II. Body	How it started: What happened: 1. 2. 3.
III. Conclusion	In the end, ...
IV. Analysis	Tell what you learned or why it was a memorable experience.

B. Using your summary, discuss your memorable experience with a partner. Provide details and information about the experience.

C. As you listen to your partner's experience, what can you infer about his / her experience? List two inferences you made by listening to your partner.

D. Discuss your inferences with each other. Were your inferences correct?

E. Work with another partner. Take turns discussing each other's memorable experiences. As you listen to your partner, politely interrupt twice to ask a question about the experience. Use the phrases in the box to the right.

Polite ways to interrupt
If I could just stop you for a moment, …
I'm sorry to interrupt, but …
I'd like to clarify something.

F. After listening to each other's presentations, take turns asking and responding to each other's polite requests for more information. Use the phrases in the box.

Self-Assessment		
Yes	**No**	
☐	☐	I successfully outlined and discussed a memorable experience.
☐	☐	I successfully made inferences about my partner's experience.
☐	☐	I was able to politely interrupt my partner.
☐	☐	I was able to make two polite requests.
☐	☐	I can pronounce three-word phrasal verbs.
☐	☐	I can correctly use the target vocabulary words from the unit.

Discussion Questions

With a partner or in a small group, discuss the following questions.

1. What does a geologist do in his / her job?
2. What makes geology a good field to study?
3. Would geology be a good field for you? Why or why not?

UNIT 8

The Happiness Formula

In this unit, you will

> learn about recent studies on income and happiness.
> increase your understanding of the target academic words for this unit.

LISTENING AND SPEAKING SKILLS

> Using Mind Maps
> Checking for Understanding
> **PRONUNCIATION** The /h/ Sound in Auxiliary Verbs

Self-Assessment

Think about how well you know each target word, and check (✓) the appropriate column. I have…

TARGET WORDS	never seen this word before.	heard or seen the word but am not sure what it means.	heard or seen the word and understand what it means.	used the word confidently in *either* speaking or writing.
AWL				
🔑 anticipate				
assess				
🔑 consult				
diminish				
🔑 economy				
evident				
format				
mature				
🔑 prior				
🔑 proportion				
psychology				
transit				

🔑 Oxford 3000™ keywords

Vocabulary Activities

Word Form Chart			
Noun	**Verb**	**Adjective**	**Adverb**
diminution	diminish	diminished	_____
economist economy	_____	economic economical	economically
evidence	evidenced	evident	evidently
proportion	_____	proportional	proportionally
psychologist psychology	_____	psychological	psychologically

A. Complete the paragraph below using the correct form of the target words in the Word Form Chart. Use the words in parentheses to help you.

Recently, in a joint endeavor, a / an _____*economist*_____
(1. person who studies the economy)

and a / an _____ studied the relationship
(2. person who studies the mind)

between happiness and income. _____,
(3. apparently)

a person's happiness is not always _____
(4. corresponding in size or degree)

to a person's income. For example, many lottery winners showed

_____ levels of happiness after becoming
(5. decreased)

rich. Also, a person's mental health is an important part of his /

her happiness. So, to be happy, we need to be doing well both

_____ and _____.
(6. in a way connected with wealth or money)   (7. in a way connected with a person's mind)

B. The word *diminish* means "to make something become smaller or weaker; to decrease." List some things that diminish your ability to focus in class. Compare your answers with a partner.

1. _*not eating breakfast*_____

2. _____

3. _____

4. _____

The word *proportion* refers to "the relationship of one thing to another in size, amount," or degree.

> A large **proportion** of our students study economics. Almost forty percent of all students study economics.

When something is disproportionate, it is too large or small when compared with something else.

> This university has a **disproportionate** number of female students. Eighty percent of the students are female.

CORPUS

C. Compare the percentage of students who majored in each subject last year and this year. Use the word *proportion* to describe the change.

Last year (majors)		This year (majors)		Change (%)
business students	30%	business students	23%	7%
economics students	34%	economics students	40%	6%
psychology students	25%	psychology students	16%	9%
geology students	11%	geology students	21%	10%
total	100%	total	100%	

1. *The proportion of business students decreased.*

2. _____

3. _____

4. _____

D. Describe each situation using the word *disproportionate*.

1. One student spends about half of the class with the teacher.

   The student spends a disproportionate share of time with the teacher.

2. One employee earns much more than anyone in the office.

   _____

3. One team member does most of the work and makes most decisions.

   _____

E. Mark each item *E* if it relates to the work of an economist. Mark it *P* if it relates to the work of a psychologist. Discuss each profession with a partner.

_P_ 1. works in a hospital or clinic   ____ 4. works in government offices

____ 2. meets with patients   ____ 5. prescribes medicine

____ 3. analyzes finances   ____ 6. uses mathematics

About the Topic

Does money make people happy? People have thought about this question for a long time. Research has shown that long-term happiness may depend less on how much money a person has and more on how he / she reacts to life events.

Before You Watch

Read these questions. Discuss your answers in a small group.

1. What do you think are the three most important factors for happiness?

2. How important is money to a person's happiness? Explain your answer.

3. What programs and policies should society focus on so that people will be happy?

Watch

Read the Listen for Main Ideas activity below. Go online to watch a BBC report on wealth and happiness. Find out if happiness research matches your ideas about what makes a person happy.

Listen for Main Ideas

Circle the correct answer to complete each sentence.

1. Research shows that when income, money, and wealth increase, happiness ____.

   a. increases a little

   b. increases a lot

   c. doesn't change or decreases a little

2. Professor Daniel Kahneman wants to know how to ____.

   a. make people happy

   b. increase incomes

   c. improve mental health

3. Consumerism promises us ____.

   a. a better understanding of others

   b. happiness, but it doesn't work

   c. happiness, and it delivers

4. The volunteers who received money showed why ____.

   a. consumerism is good

   b. comparison makes us less happy

   c. comparison makes us happier

LEARN

A *mind map* is a way to take notes that will help you to remember and think about important information from a lecture or presentation. To make a mind map, write the topic or main idea in a circle at the center of the page. Add lines and drawings to connect supporting details and key words to the main idea.

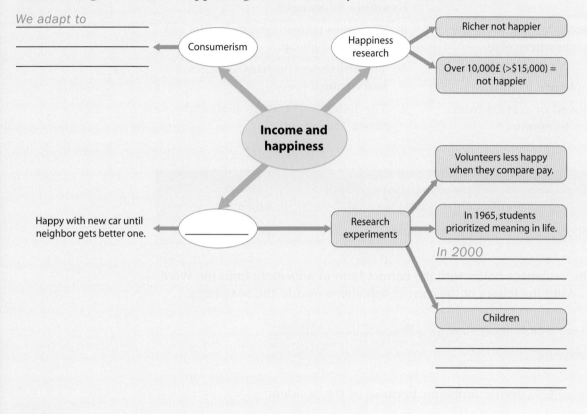

APPLY

A. Work in a small group. Look at the mind map above. What is the topic or main idea of the BBC report?

_____

B. Go online to watch the first part of the video again and add to the mind map.

C. Go online to watch the second part of the video again. Add details, examples, and information to your mind map. Compare your mind map with a partner, and add information that you missed.

D. Exchange your mind map with a partner. Using your partner's mind map, discuss two of the main ideas or other important information from the BBC report.

Vocabulary Activities

A. The word *transit* has multiple meanings. Match the dictionary definitions on the left with the example sentences on the right.

Definitions

<u>c</u> 1. going through a place on the way to somewhere else

___ 2. the system of buses and trains that people use to travel

___ 3. being moved or carried from one place to another

Example Sentences

a. The mass transit system in this city is fast and cheap.

b. The shipping company charges a hefty transit fee.

c. The letter is in transit. It should arrive tomorrow.

Word Form Chart		
Noun	**Verb**	**Adjective**
anticipation	anticipate	anticipated

B. Complete the sentences below with the correct form of *anticipate* from the Word Form Chart. Write the letters of the correct definitions next to the sentences.

a. to think with excitement about something that is going to happen

b. to expect something

<u>b</u> 1. We ___anticipate___ traffic problems because of the accident.

___ 2. Experts _____ an increase in rain this year. There may be flooding, too.

___ 3. The host family waited in _____ for the arrival of the student. It was an exciting day.

___ 4. The movie was the most highly _____ film of the year. Everyone was waiting for it.

___ 5. We _____ big changes next year. It is going to be a difficult time.

C. *Consult* means "to go to someone for information or advice." Work with a partner. Discuss who or what you would consult in each situation.

1. You want to know your score on a test.
2. You are feeling sick.
3. You want the definition of a word.
4. You have a legal problem.
5. You want career advice.

Prior means "happening before something else." The phrase *prior to* + (verb-*ing*) is often used with *prior*.

> **Prior to** *leaving for China, I packed two large suitcases.*

We also use the phrase *prior to* + (noun).

> **Prior to** *this trip, I had never been to a foreign country.*

CORPUS

D. Complete the following sentences.

1. Prior to taking this class, I had never met _____*my teacher*_____.

2. Prior to this class, I had never heard the word _____.

3. Prior to attending this university, I had not studied _____.

One meaning for *mature* is "to develop emotionally and start to behave like a sensible adult."

> *Having a part-time job helps a person to* **mature**.

CORPUS

E. Work with a partner. Discuss events in your lives that have helped you mature. What other types of events help young people mature?

> *Living on my own has helped me mature.*

F. The word *format* refers to "the general arrangement, plan, or design of something." Discuss the format for each item below with a partner.

1. Look through this book. What is the format of each unit?

> *Each unit begins with an opener page. The second page has a vocabulary activity.*

2. Describe the format of your school's website.

_____

3. What is the format for the operating system on your computer?

_____

G. *Assessment* refers to "the act of judging or forming an opinion about someone or something." How does the teacher academically *assess* you in this class? List three different kinds of assessments related to your grade in this class.

1. ___*the final exam*___   2. _____   3. _____

About the Topic

Study abroad programs are growing at many universities around the world. Studying abroad gives students a chance to experience a new culture, learn a foreign language, and travel.

Before You Watch

Read these questions. Discuss your answers in a small group.

1. What are some good ways for a person to learn about a foreign culture?
2. If you had an opportunity to study abroad, where would you go? Why?
3. How important is studying abroad for a university student?

Watch

Read the Listen for Main Ideas activity below. Go online to watch an interview with a student who shares his experience of studying abroad and talks about his university's Study Abroad Program.

Listen for Main Ideas

Read the questions about the video. Work with a partner to ask and answer these questions.

1. Where did the student go to study? *China*
2. Where did he live while he studied abroad?
3. What did he enjoy learning about?
4. What was the best part of this student's trip?

SPEAKING SKILL Checking for Understanding

LEARN

When you check for understanding, you restate what you have heard in your own words. Checking for understanding is a good way to: (1) check if you have understood correctly, (2) highlight important points, and (3) clarify details.

Checking for understanding
So you think that it is a good idea.
So you're saying that it is a good idea.
If I understand you correctly, you are recommending homestays.
Let me make sure that I understand. You are recommending homestays.

After checking for understanding, you will often want to ask follow-up questions to get more information.

Follow-up questions
Then how about the cost of the program?
How was your overall experience?
Is there anything else you would recommend?
What do you think about living in the dorms?

APPLY

A. Discuss the statements below with a partner. Use different *checking for understanding* phrases from the chart on page 92.

1. With the world becoming more interconnected, studying abroad is a very important experience for university students to have.

   So you are saying that studying abroad is useful for university students.

2. For me, learning about cultural customs improved my understanding of China and the people there.

3. The format for each program includes trips, events, and other opportunities.

B. Work with a partner. What follow-up question would you ask for each statement in activity A? Use the chart above to help you.

   Is there any specific program that you would recommend?

C. Watch the video again. Fill in the chart below. Check your answers as a class.

Checking for understanding	Follow-up questions
1. So _____you thought_____ that the study abroad program in China matched your academic goals.	2. Then how _____ your classes there?
3. _____ that the Study Abroad Office organized your homestay.	4. _____ that?
5. _____ , you're saying homestays are a great way to learn the local language.	6. Then _____ that surprised you about the culture?
7. So _____ that I understand. If someone offers me something in China, I should refuse it several times before I accept it?	

D. Look at the *checking for understanding* phrases in Apply, activity C. Discuss some other follow-up questions that you could ask for 2, 4, and 6. Share your questions with the class.

LEARN

A. When you form a contraction with the auxiliary verbs *has*, *have*, or *had*, you often drop the /h/ sound and the vowel sound. This means a syllable disappears. Go online to listen to the examples.

Pronoun / noun + *has*	he's, she's, it's, Pat's, Ann's, the weather's
Pronoun + *have*	I've, you've, we've, they've
Pronoun + *had*	I'd, you'd, he'd, she'd, we'd, they'd

B. When you form a contraction with a modal plus *have*, *have* is reduced. Sometimes you drop the /h/ sound. Other times, *have* becomes the /ə/ sound. Go online to listen to the examples.

could have	a) could've	b) coulda
would have	a) would've	b) woulda
should have	a) should've	b) shoulda

C. Go online to listen to the following sentences.

Where h̸as Tom been?	Where /z/ Tom been?
Where h̸ad she been?	Where /d/ she been?
Jackie and Tom h̸ave been traveling this semester.	Jackie and Tom /əv/ been traveling this semester.
Tom h̸ad read the chapter for the test but didn't understand it.	Tom /əd/ read the chapter for the test but didn't understand it.
It h̸ad been easier to travel where I knew the language than where I didn't.	It /əd/ been easier to travel where I knew the language than where I didn't.
It would be boring to travel alone.	It /əd/ be boring to travel alone.

APPLY

A. Go online to listen to some sentences. Put a check (✓) in the column of the auxiliary verb that you hear.

	Has	Have	Had
1.	✓		
2.			
3.			
4.			
5.			

B. Go online to listen to the sentences with contractions or reductions. Fill in the full forms of *has*, *have*, *had*, *could have*, *would have*, or *should have*. Listen to the audio one more time to check your answers. Then practice making contractions or reductions with a partner.

1. I ___*have*___ been wanting a raise, but I don't think it'll change how happy I am.

2. Prior to studying in England, he _____ taken several English classes.

3. You _____ seen the new format for the project, right?

4. She _____ made more money but she decided to keep the job she liked.

5. We _____ done the research but the findings still surprised us.

6. Saving more money is what we _____ done if we wanted to take a vacation.

C. With a partner, talk about memories that make you happy. Use the auxiliary verbs *has*, *have*, and *had* in your description, and include contractions and reductions.

End of Unit Task

Practice the skills you have learned in this unit by preparing, presenting, and listening to a presentation. Draw a mind map of your partner's presentation. As you listen, check for understanding and ask follow-up questions.

A. Prepare a short presentation about one of the following:

- a career that you are interested in
- a study abroad program that you would like to participate in
- a country that you know a lot about

I. Introduction

1. Greet your audience. Say what your topic is.

2. Tell your audience how many points you will make.

II. Body

1. Introduce each point using clear signal phrases as you move from point to point.

2. Give examples and supporting information under each point. Use facts, statistics, quotations, specific examples, etc.

III. Conclusion

1. Tell your audience what you've said by summarizing your main points.

2. Thank your audience and take questions.

B. Work with a partner. Listen to each other's short presentations. As you listen, create a mind map.

C. Find out more information about your partner's presentation and add to your mind map by checking for understanding. Use phrases from the box on page 92.

D. Prepare two follow-up questions to ask your partner. Then add to your mind map again.

E. Work with another partner. Using the mind map that you created, take turns discussing the presentations that you first listened to.

Self-Assessment		
Yes	**No**	
☐	☐	I successfully prepared a short presentation.
☐	☐	I successfully drew a mind map.
☐	☐	I was able to check for understanding.
☐	☐	I was able to ask follow-up questions.
☐	☐	I can drop the /h/ sound in auxiliary verbs.
☐	☐	I can correctly use the target vocabulary words from the unit.

Discussion Questions

With a partner or in a small group, discuss the following questions.

1. Why don't possessions make people happy?

2. What does make people happy?

3. Where would you go to be happy?

UNIT
9

Stop the Presses

In this unit, you will
> learn about changes in the newspaper industry.
> increase your understanding of the target academic words for this unit.

LISTENING AND SPEAKING SKILLS
> Facts and Opinions
> Being Persuasive in Academic Discussions
> **PRONUNCIATION** Common Reductions

Self-Assessment
Think about how well you know each target word, and check (✓) the appropriate column. I have…

TARGET WORDS	never seen this word before.	heard or seen the word but am not sure what it means.	heard or seen the word and understand what it means.	used the word confidently in *either* speaking or writing.
AWL				
🔑 brief				
controversy				
🔑 drama				
ignorance				
🔑 impact				
🔑 investigate				
🔑 overall				
🔑 policy				
🔑 rely				
scope				
so-called				
🔑 survive				

🔑 Oxford 3000™ keywords

Vocabulary Activities

Word Form Chart			
Noun	**Verb**	**Adjective**	**Adverb**
drama	dramatize	dramatic	dramatically
investigation investigator	investigate	investigative	_____
survival survivor	survive	_____	_____

A. Complete the paragraph below using the correct form of the target words in the Word Form Chart. Use the words in parentheses to help you.

Last night, I watched a ____drama____ on television. It was about a journalist
                   (3. serious play)

who _____ stories and events around his city. He interviewed
  (2. finds out information)

sources for each of his stories. Then I watched a news report about

the _____ rescue and _____ of a man who was lost at
 (3. exciting and impressive)   (4. staying alive)

sea. The man talked about what he did to _____, and the report
                             (5. stay alive)

also _____ similar stories about _____ at sea.
  (6. examined)   (7. the state of continuing to live)

B. The word *survive* can refer to (a) a challenging situation. It can also refer to (b) life or death situations. Write the letter of the meaning used in each sentence.

_a_ 1. The team survived a difficult round of events.

___ 2. I survived all of my final examinations.

___ 3. The building collapsed during the earthquake, but everyone survived.

___ 4. The patient survived the deadly disease.

C. The word *scope* has multiple meanings and forms. Match the dictionary definitions on the left with the example sentences on the right.

Definitions

_c_ 1. to look at or examine carefully

___ 2. an instrument for looking through or watching something with

___ 3. the range things that a subject or activity deals with

Example Sentences

a. The new scope helped the scientists see the tiny bacteria.

b. The professor explained the scope of the new math class.

c. She scoped out the place before entering because it was dark inside.

D. Discuss the following questions regarding *investigate* with a partner.

1. Why would a detective investigate police evidence?

2. Who would investigate ancient pottery and old tools? Why?

3. Why would a newspaper company investigate the cause of lost sales?

a. *So-called* is used to introduce a word or phrase that people usually use to describe someone or something.

*Readers will have to start paying a **so-called** micro-payment, which is a small fee.*

b. *So-called* is also used to show that you do not think a word or phrase being used to describe someone or something is appropriate.

*These **so-called** "smart people" could not even solve easy problems.*

CORPUS

E. Write the letter (a or b) for the meaning of *so-called* in each sentence.

_a_ 1. The world is becoming very well connected. The so-called global village that we live in lets people meet and connect with each other very easily.

___ 2. The so-called "investigative journalist" was actually getting his information by copying it from other websites.

___ 3. The so-called "large income difference" was much smaller than what the presenter claimed it would be.

F. The word *overall* means "including everything or everyone; in total." Complete the following sentences with your overall impression of each aspect of campus life.

1. Overall, the food on campus is _____*cheap and good*_____.

2. Overall, the people on campus are _____.

3. Overall, this course is _____.

About the Topic

Because of the Internet, the newspaper industry is changing quickly. More people are reading the news online instead of buying newspapers. The Internet has also raised the question of who owns information. When a news blog uses stories from a newspaper, is it stealing?

Before You Watch

Read these questions. Discuss your answers in a small group.

1. Where do you usually get your news (a blog, a newspaper, a magazine)?

2. Do you prefer reading news online or in a newspaper?

3. How do you think people will get their news ten or twenty years in the future?

Watch

Read the Listen for Main Ideas activity below. Go online to watch a video about the problems and challenges that newspapers are facing. Will printed newspapers survive into the future?

Listen for Main Ideas

Go online to watch the first part of the video. Mark each sentence as *T* (true) or *F* (false). Work with a partner. Restate false sentences to make them correct.

_T_ 1. The report says that newspapers can't survive without change.

___ 2. Michael Wolf thinks that the newspaper business is failing.

___ 3. Many newspapers are losing money.

___ 4. Classified ads are still popular in print.

___ 5. News websites are updated constantly.

LISTENING SKILL   Facts and Opinions

LEARN

A *fact* is something that is true. A fact can be proved.

> *Last year, our company's sales increased by five percent.*

An opinion is someone's feelings or thoughts about something. Here are three different ways to express opinions:

1. Opinion phrases: *I think, I argue, I believe, In my opinion, For me, In my view*

   For us, the system is perfect.   **In my opinion**, the proposal will work.

   I believe this is our best chance.   **He argues** that the system will work.

2. Adverbs and adjectives

   This project is **terrible**.   That building is **beautiful**.

   They work too **slowly**.

3. Doubt or probability phrases: *might, maybe, perhaps, probably, possibly, could, can*

It **might** be a good idea.   The idea **could** be useful.

Maybe we should help him.

APPLY

A. Work with a partner. Look at the statements. Write *O* for opinion and *F* for fact. For the opinion sentences, underline the words or phrases that show an opinion.

_F_ 1. After nearly 150 years, the *Rocky Mountain News* printed its final newspaper.

____ 2. Newspapers might not survive without dramatic change.

____ 3. I believe that it's the end of the newspaper business right now.

____ 4. Since 2000, daily newspaper circulation has decreased from 55 million to 50 million.

____ 5. Bloggers steal stories from newspapers, and it is really terrible.

B. Go online to watch the second part of the video. Fill in the blanks. Then write *O* for opinion and *F* for fact.

1. Brian Tierney and a consortium of wealthy investors bought the 180-year-old *Philadelphia Inquirer* and the tabloid *Daily News* some ___three years ago___ .	1. _F_
2. Not _____ money, given the overall scope of what television bills and cell phone bills and all the rest of it are … And _____ people will pay it.	2. ____
3. Right now Brian Tierney's company _____.	3. ____
4. He _____ that if the people who read the *Inquirer* pay for it with a higher newsstand price and a subscriber fee on the web, the enterprise will survive and flourish.	4. ____

C. What do you think? Is it wrong for news blogs to use information and stories that they find in printed newspapers? Discuss your opinions in a small group.

Vocabulary Activities

Word Form Chart		
Noun	**Adjective**	**Adverb**
brief	brief	briefly
controversy	controversial	controversially
ignorance	ignorant	_____
reliability	reliable	reliably

A. Complete the sentences below using the correct form of the target words in the Word Form Chart. Use the words in parentheses to help you.

1. Could you give us a _____*brief*_____ explanation of the plan? It should be no
                   (short)
   more than one minute.

2. Some bloggers are _____ of rules for reporting the news. They do not
           (not having information or knowledge)
   know them very well.

3. The _____ started because bloggers were using other people's stories.
     (strong disagreement)
   People continue to debate the issue.

4. The reporter found a _____ person who knew the facts of the
          (able to be trusted)
   situation.

B. Read the different class policies listed below. With a partner, discuss how these policies compare with your class policies.

> 1. There is a strict policy against cheating on exams.
>
> 2. Students may not use smartphones in the classroom.
>
> 3. Any student who arrives more than ten minutes late is marked as *absent*.
>
> 4. All students must bring the class textbook to each lecture.

C. *Controversial* means causing a lot of strong disagreement and discussion. How controversial are the following issues in your state or country? Add one of your own issues. Discuss in a small group.

Issues	Highly controversial	Somewhat controversial	Not controversial
government policies for helping homeless people			✓
illegal downloading of movies and music			
animal testing in making new medicines			
_____			

The word *impact* means "the powerful effect that [someone or] something has on someone or something" else.

> *Getting my first job had a big **impact** on me. It taught me about hard work and saving money.* (thing impacts a person)

> *My father has had a big **impact** on me. He has taught me so much about life.* (person impacts a person)

D. Fill out the chart. What impact did the following events and people have on you? Add two events or people of your own. Discuss your answers with a partner.

Events / people	Big impact	Small impact	No impact	No experience
getting your first job	✓			
taking a trip abroad				
your best friend				
a family member				
_____				
_____				

About the Topic

Imagine a volcano has just erupted. It would take time for news organizations to send their professional reporters to the location to take photos and interview people there. However, what if someone in the town used a smartphone camera to report the event? This is one aspect of citizen journalism. Citizen journalism is when regular people, or citizens, help to report the news.

Before You Listen

Read these questions. Discuss your answers in a small group.

1. Is reporting the news an interesting occupation? Would you like to become a citizen journalist?

2. Some people believe that citizen journalists are more likely than professional reporters to make mistakes when reporting the news. Should only professional journalists report the news?

3. Do you read the student newspaper on campus? What do you think of it?

Listen

Read the Listen for Main Ideas activity below. Go online to listen to two students discuss their opinions on citizen journalism. Does citizen journalism improve the news we get? Or should news stories only come from professional reporters?

Listen for Main Ideas

Mark each sentence as *T* (true) or *F* (false). Work with a partner. Restate false sentences to make them correct.

_T_ 1. Citizen journalism involves regular people finding, reporting, and delivering the news.

___ 2. Citizen journalism is too narrow and limited.

___ 3. Both students agree that, overall, citizen journalism is a positive thing.

___ 4. Most news organizations make their own special rules or policies for reporting the news.

___ 5. Sometimes citizen journalists cover stories that the main news organizations ignore.

SPEAKING SKILL Being Persuasive in Academic Discussions

LEARN

Being persuasive in academic discussion means that you try to get someone to believe or agree with your opinion. One way you can do this is by first stating a point against your opinion. Then you explain why you disagree with that point.

1. State a point <u>against</u> your opinion.	Some people may think that paying small fees to read articles online will help newspapers earn money.
2. Explain why you disagree with the point.	However, this is not true. Research shows that news organizations lost many readers after charging small fees. Some of those organizations went out of business.

APPLY

A. Read the incomplete statements below. Then listen and fill in the blanks.

1. I know that people _____ *might say* _____ that citizen journalism is good because it gets the average person more involved in the news, but I _____.
   The average person doesn't have the skills of a professional reporter.

2. I know _____ that citizen journalists are ignorant of the rules of journalism, but _____ that bloggers and independent reporters are starting to follow those rules.

B. Work with a partner. Which of the points below do you disagree with? First, state the point you disagree with. Then explain why you disagree with each point.

Issue	Point	Point
University students shouldn't be required to take two years of language courses.	Two years of language courses will help students get better jobs.	Some students do not need language skills for their major or future careers.

Some people think that not every student needs language skills for their future careers. However, ...

C. Work in a small group. Think of a controversial international, domestic, or campus issue.

Issue: _____

D. What is your opinion of the issue your group selected? Take a moment to think of a point someone else might make against your opinion. Then explain why you disagree with that point.

Point against your opinion: _____

_____

Why you disagree with the point against your opinion: _____

E. Work in a small group. Discuss your opinion of the issue your group selected.

PRONUNCIATION SKILL Common Reductions

LEARN

A. When speaking, you often reduce common phrases. Go online to listen to examples of reduced forms of a verb + *to*.

Original form	Reduced form	Example
has to	*hasta*	hasta ⌃ He has to finish the article.
have to	*hafta*	hafta ⌃ The journalists have to write about the controversy.
want to	*wanna*	wanna ⌃ Do you want to read this?
wants to	*wansta*	wansta ⌃ Who wants to become a journalist?
going to	*gonna*	gonna ⌃ I'm going to buy a newspaper.
supposed to	*sposta* *saposta*	sposta ⌃ The new policy is supposed to help the industry.

B. Go online to listen to examples of verb + *me*.

Original Form	Contracted Form	Example
let me	*lemme*	Lemme ⌃ Let me borrow that.
give me	*gimme*	Gimme ⌃ Give me your advice.

APPLY

A. Go online to listen to the sentences. Fill in the original form of the reduction that you hear. Then repeat the sentences.

1. Bloggers don't ____*have to*____ follow the same rules as professional journalists.

2. Journalists aren't _____ report rumors.

3. _____ the URL for where you read your news online.

4. _____ give you my resources for finding updated news stories.

5. The impact of citizen journalism _____ affect newspaper sales.

6. As a citizen journalist, he _____ offer a different perspective.

7. The reporter is _____ investigate the controversy.

B. With a partner, discuss the difference between being a kid and being an adult. What responsibilities do adults have that kids don't? Use reductions in your answer.

                        hafta

A: When I was a kid, I didn't have to worry about money.

         hasta

B: My son only has to do his homework and his chores. But he always

    wansta

wants to do other things.

End of Unit Task

To review the skills you learned in this unit, listen to a lecture on objectivity and journalism. Identify facts and opinions related to the issue. Then discuss your opinion by stating points against your opinion and why you disagree with those points.

A. Go online to listen to Dr. Jerome Tyler discuss objectivity in journalism. Fill in the blanks below.

News reporters should not give their opinions.	News reporters should give their opinions.
1. a reporter's job is to report the facts	1. reporters understand the stories _____
2. let people decide what they _____ *think*	2. it is impossible to be _____
3. people can watch a debate or read an _____	3. reporters should be honest about what they really _____

B. Work with a partner. Discuss the facts below. Which side of the debate could each of the facts below support?

Opinion news shows have increased in the past ten years.

Research shows that online news reports with opinions receive more views than reports without opinions.

An international survey showed that the majority of people want their news to be "fair and accurate."

The definition of *report* is "to [collect and] present a written or spoken account of an event."

C. Work in a group of six. Then divide into two groups of three students each. Assign one group to agree with the statement below. Assign the other group to disagree with the statement below.

Reporters should be objective in their reporting of the news.

D. In your group of three, look at the points against your opinion in the chart on page 107. Choose two points against your opinion. Then write down why you disagree with those points.

Points against your opinion	Why you disagree with those points
1.	1.
2.	2.

E. Discuss the statement with the other group of three. Support the side you were assigned to for activities C and D.

Self-Assessment		
Yes	**No**	
☐	☐	I successfully listened to different points related to objectivity in journalism.
☐	☐	I successfully identified facts and the opinions they support.
☐	☐	I successfully explained why I disagree with different points.
☐	☐	I was persuasive in discussing my opinion of objectivity in journalism.
☐	☐	I can reduce common phrases.
☐	☐	I can correctly use the target vocabulary words from the unit.

Discussion Questions

With a partner or in a small group, discuss the following questions.

1. How have the Internet and citizen journalism changed the way we get news?
2. Do you think the news we get today is as good as it was in the past? Why or why not?
3. What are the best qualities in a journalist?

UNIT 10

Artificial Retina

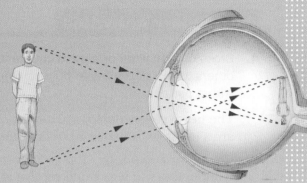

In this unit, you will

> learn about the development of artificial retinas for the blind.
> increase your understanding of the target academic words for this unit.

LISTENING AND SPEAKING SKILLS

> Using Context to Follow a Lecture
> Nonverbal Communication
> PRONUNCIATION Contrastive and Emphatic Stress

Self-Assessment

Think about how well you know each target word, and check (✓) the appropriate column. I have...

TARGET WORDS	never seen this word before.	heard or seen the word but am not sure what it means.	heard or seen the word and understand what it means.	used the word confidently in *either* speaking or writing.
AWL				
academy				
correspond				
🔑 generation				
🔑 indicate				
🔑 occur				
🔑 perspective				
🔑 phase				
🔑 potential				
🔑 principal				
🔑 range				
🔑 restore				
🔑 technology				

🔑 Oxford 3000™ keywords

Vocabulary Activities

A. Cross out the word or phrase in parentheses with a different meaning from the others. Use a dictionary to help you understand new words. Compare answers with a partner.

1. The next (*generation of / phase for / stage or step for / ~~research for~~*) artificial arms and legs is expected to be highly advanced.

2. (*Possibly / Potentially / It is certain that / There is a chance that*) people without arms or legs could receive artificial legs or arms that are faster and stronger than human ones are.

3. The FDA, or Food and Drug Administration, is an organization that regulates new medicine. The FDA has approved new artificial legs that (*delay / restore / bring back / return to a previous condition*) a person's ability to walk or run.

4. From a disabled patient's perspective, the artificial (*processes / advanced equipment / scientific knowledge or machinery / technology*) for legs and arms is a gift that allows people to live a normal life.

B. For the target words in bold, match each dictionary definition on the left with the correct example sentence on the right.

Definitions

_c_ 1. a phase or stage in the development of a product or machine

____ 2. a group of people of similar age involved in a particular activity

____ 3. the average time in which children grow up, become adults, and have their own children

____ 4. the production of something, especially electricity or heat

Example Sentences

a. The **generation** of green energy was the main purpose of the technology.

b. The younger **generation** has different ideas than the older **generation** does.

c. The most recent **generation** of tablet computers has many new features.

d. Our family has lived in the same home for many **generations**.

Definitions

____ 1. to bring back a situation or feeling that existed before

____ 2. to bring someone or something back to a former condition, place, or position

____ 3. to repair a building, piece of furniture, or work of art so that it looks as good as it did originally

Example Sentences

a. The government **restored** the historic building.

b. The good news has helped to **restore** confidence in the economy.

c. The medicine helped **restore** the patient to good health.

Perspective refers to the way you think about something or your point of view.

> From my **perspective**, the artificial retina seemed like a great opportunity. However, my friend thought that it might be dangerous.

When you *put things in perspective* or *keep things in perspective*, you recognize what is really important and what is not important in a particular situation.

> When the child cried about having to wear glasses, his mother told him to **put things in perspective** and be thankful that he was not blind.

CORPUS

C. Fill out the chart below. Add one of your own topics to the list. Discuss your answers with a small group.

	Always about one's perspective	Sometimes about one's perspective	Never about one's perspective
Success in life	✓		
General well-being and health			
The quality of a movie or book			
_____			

> I think success in life is always related to a person's perspective. For example, some people think success is about money, but other people think that it is about being happy.

D. What are some things you have to remind yourself to keep in perspective? Discuss your answers with a partner.

1. _Sometimes I complain that I don't have much money, but I have to keep this in perspective. Many people are much poorer than I am._

2. _____

3. _____

About the Topic

Medical technology can help people in incredible ways. Scientists and doctors have developed small machines that can replace body parts. When these machines are surgically attached, patients who have lost a limb or even their vision can regain some of the functions of their body parts that are missing or that no longer work.

Before You Watch

Read these questions. Discuss your answers in a small group.

1. What is a good doctor?

2. What is one of the most important recent medical breakthroughs? Why is it important?

3. How are medical practices in the United States different from medical practices in other countries?

Watch

Read the Listen for Main Ideas activity below. Go online to watch a report on the development of artificial retinas for blind people. The report tells about one man who has had an artificial retina implanted in his eye.

Listen for Main Ideas

Work with a partner. Discuss each sentence and circle the correct answer based on the video.

1. The artificial retina ____.

   a. gives people perfect vision

   b. does not work yet

   c. helps people regain some of their vision

2. Dean Lloyd ____.

   a. received an implanted chip

   b. received a completely new eye

   c. had laser surgery

3. After receiving the eye implant, Dean Lloyd ____.

   a. has almost perfect vision

   b. is able to see shapes and outlines

   c. can tell the difference between most colors

4. Dean Lloyd's daughter, Lisa ____.

   a. has the same disease as her father

   b. has normal vision

   c. will not become blind

5. ____ could benefit from artificial retinas.

   a. A small number of people

   b. Many people

   c. Only people who were born blind

LEARN

Context refers to the words that come before and after a word, phrase, or statement that helps you understand it. When you hear a word that you do not know, listen to the context around the word it appears within. This will help you understand the word. Most importantly, stay focused on the general ideas.

APPLY

A. First read the sentences below. Then go online to watch part of the report. As you watch, match the words on the left with the context on the right.

1. artificial retina _b_
2. clinical trial ___
3. hereditary ___

a. volunteers for surgical implant
b. can help sightless regain vision
c. the same disease her father has

B. Work with a partner. Use context clues to guess the meanings of the words in bold below.

1. Direct sunlight can damage your **retina** and cause vision problems.

   The retina helps people see.

2. For the **clinical trial** of the new drug, the company chose a group of sick people that could benefit from the drug.

3. His father and grandfather had the same disease. This was not surprising because the disease is **hereditary**.

C. Use the context clues in activities A and B to complete these sentences with the correct definition.

_a_ 1. Your retina is the part of your eye that ___.
   a. receives images
   b. controls size

___ 2. A clinical trial is ___.
   a. the first part of a medical test
   b. a medical test on humans

___ 3. A hereditary disease is one that was ___.
   a. contracted by chance
   b. passed from parents to children

Vocabulary Activities

Word Form Chart		
Noun	**Verb**	**Adjective**
academy	_____	academic
correspondence	correspond	corresponding
indication	indicate	indicative
occurrence	occur	_____
range	range	_____

A. Complete the paragraph below using the correct form of the target words in the Word Form Chart. Use the words in parentheses to help you.

Recent _____ *academic* _____ research _____
       (1. connected with education, studying)   (2. to show that something is true)

that living in a clean environment can lead to increases in life expectancy.

The _____ of Sciences also did research on this
    (3. school or college for special training)

issue. Their work showed that cleaner air _____
                                    (4. matched)

with higher life expectancy. Thus, the _____ of
                             (5. happening or existence)

pollution may lead to shorter lives. The academic researchers studied a

wide _____ of cities around the world to come up
           (6. variety)

with their data.

The adjective *principal* means "the most important" or "the main."

    The **principal** reason for the increase was new medical technology.

As a noun, the word *principal* refers to the person who is in charge of a school.

    The **principal** gave a speech at the graduation ceremony.

The word *principal* is often confused with *principle*, which refers to a general truth or rule.

    Each medical school student had his / her own **principles** for being a good doctor.

CORPUS

B. Complete the sentences with *principal* or *principle*.

1. The doctor's ___*principal*___ advice was to be positive.

2. The _____ reason for the group's success was their creativity.

3. The professor outlined several mathematical _____ for the students to memorize.

4. The course teaches the basic _____ of medicine.

5. The _____ called all the teachers together to discuss the new year.

C. A *phase* is a stage in a process of change or development. Fill in the blanks with the phrases in the box that best describe each scenario.

the first phase / the final phase / the second phase / the preliminary phase

The different phases in development of a new drug:

___*the final phase*___ 1. All of the clinical trials revealed positive results. We are almost ready to bring the product to the market.

_____ 2. We are doing the first test tomorrow.

_____ 3. Before we begin experimenting, we need to do some research.

_____ 4. Now that the first test is finished, we can move forward with the next experiment.

D. *Correspond* has multiple meanings. For each sentence below, write the letter of the correct definition of *correspond*.

a. to communicate by exchanging email or letters   c. to have a similar function

b. to be the same as or match something

__*a*__ 1. We correspond by email when I am overseas.

____ 2. That number does not correspond to the one in our system. The two numbers should be the same, but they are not.

____ 3. The results of the research correspond with the conclusions of the other research project.

____ 4. The Office of Abroad Studies at my university corresponds to the Office of International Studies at your university. Both offices coordinate programs for studying abroad.

About the Topic

In the past century, life expectancy has increased about 30 years for both men and women. Some experts have even claimed that because of medical technology, the youngest generation of children could live as long as 150 years.

Before You Watch

Read these questions. Discuss your answers in a small group.

1. How high do you think life expectancy will reach for your generation? Explain your answer.

2. What do you think are the keys to living a long life?

3. As people live longer, how should society adapt? What changes should we make?

Watch

Read the Listen for Main Ideas activity below. Go online to watch a student discuss life expectancy. He talks about the changes that led to dramatic increases in the lengths of our lives.

Listen for Main Ideas

Go online to watch the video. Mark each sentence as *T* (true) or *F* (false). Work with a partner. Restate false sentences to make them correct.

_F_ 1. In the 1800s, every country's life expectancy was over 40. *It was under 40.*

____ 2. Today, average life expectancy is around 70 years of age.

____ 3. In the 1900s, increases in life expectancy were mostly because of cures for deadly diseases.

____ 4. Experts believe life expectancy will decrease in the future.

____ 5. Today, one of the biggest challenges is to help people live longer.

PRESENTATION SKILL Nonverbal Communication

LEARN

Nonverbal communication refers to hand gestures, posture, eye contact, facial expressions, and tone of voice. According to some experts, nonverbal communication accounts for up to 70 percent of what is communicated.

Hand gestures	Posture	Eye contact	Facial expressions	Tone of voice
Move your hands to express ideas and add emphasis	Stand tall and straight with your feet firmly on the floor	Look at your listeners' eyes for 2–3 seconds at a time	Use appropriate facial movements to communicate, such as smiling	Vary your voice level; slightly raise your voice to emphasize important points and ideas

APPLY

A. Go online to watch the student's first presentation, given before he received feedback from his instructor on using nonverbal signals in a presentation. Which nonverbal signals below did he do correctly? In the boxes below, write the number you think best applies: 1 = excellent, 2 = OK, or 3 = needs improvement. Discuss your answers as a class.

Hand gestures	Posture	Eye contact	Facial expressions	Tone of voice
3				

B. Go online to watch the student's second presentation, after he received feedback from his instructor on using nonverbal signals when giving a presentation. In the boxes below, write the number you think best applies: *1 = excellent, 2 = OK, or 3 = needs improvement.* Discuss your answers as a class.

Hand gestures	Posture	Eye contact	Facial expressions	Tone of voice

C. What is your opinion of the health care system in the United States? Prepare a short explanation of your opinion (less than one minute).

D. Work with a partner. Take turns explaining your opinion. As you listen to your partner, write the number you think best applies to his / her presentation: 1 = excellent, 2 = OK, or 3 = needs improvement.

Hand gestures	Posture	Eye contact	Facial expressions	Tone of voice

PRONUNCIATION SKILL | Contrastive and Emphatic Stress

LEARN

In sentences, the focus words, or the most important words in each chunk, receive the stress. There are three different ways to use focus words: to introduce new information, to create contrast, and to show emphasis.

A. Go online to listen to the sentences that introduce new information. Notice the stressed focus words in each chunk.

> 1. He became a lawyer | and opened his own practice.
> 2. These increases indicate | that the world is continuing | to get healthier.

B. You use contrastive stress when you want to show contrast, or show a difference between two things, when you speak. You often use this type of stress when you are correcting someone. Go online to listen to the following sentences.

> 1. I didn't say to take the coffee; I said to make the coffee.
> 2. She said Saturday would be better, not Friday.
> 3. That's my perspective. What's your perspective?

C. You usually use emphatic stress when you want to emphasize your feelings. Some common adverbs that are used in emphatic stress are *really, incredibly, extremely, so,* and *especially*. Go online to listen.

> 1. That test was **haaard**!
> 2. I had a **haaard** day.
> 3. It is **extreeemely** cold.
> 4. His car is **sooo** fast!

APPLY

A. Go online to listen to the sentences. Underline the stressed words.

1. <u>My</u> life expectancy will be different from my <u>grandparents</u>' life expectancy.
2. The incident occurred Wednesday, not Monday.
3. His generation is more likely to own a house than her generation.
4. Did the daughter receive the surgery, or the father?
5. The study indicates a positive result, not a negative one.

B. Go online to listen to the sentences. Circle the word that has special emphasis.

1. That's (exciting) technology!
2. The range of scores is huge.
3. Corresponding with the scientist is really helpful for my paper.
4. This phase of treatment seems to be taking forever.
5. We are all incredibly lucky to have this medical care available to us.

C. Go online to listen to the sentences. Cross out and correct the mistakes.

1. Please come on ~~Saturday~~. *Sunday*
2. That's her perspective.
3. The event will occur next week.
4. The academy will approve the project.

D. Use contrastive stress to correct the sentences from activity C.

Sorry, I meant to say, "Please come on Sunday," not Saturday.

E. With a partner, create sentences to describe yourself, but change one piece of information to make them untrue. Your partner will try to guess the correct information. Use both contrastive and emphatic stress in your answers.

End of Unit Task

In this unit, you learned to listen for context to determine the meaning of words you do not know. Practice this skill by listening to another student presentation. Then give a presentation of your own to practice good nonverbal communication skills.

A. Go online to listen to a student presentation. Fill in the context related to the vocabulary words below.

Difficult words	Context
placebo	sick patients—given a pill, told _____*it was medicine*_____
	looked and tasted like real medicine but _____ real medicine
	83% of patients who took false medicine → felt better
neuropeptides	_____ produced by the brain when it thinks
	these chemicals are found all over the body
	these _____ can fight cancer and help with other health problems

B. Choose the best meaning of each word, using the context in the chart on page 119.

1. placebo

   a. a new drug

   b. a medicine that it is not real

   c. a drug with strong physical effects

2. neuropeptides

   a. chemicals produced by the brain

   b. chemicals produced by the body

   c. chemicals caused by health problems

C. Choose one of the following topics for a short presentation.

1. The connection of the mind to the body

2. Medical tourism

3. A new medical cure or technology

D. Use the outline on page 69, in Unit 6, to prepare your short presentation.

E. Work in a small group to give and watch short presentations.

1. Before you begin, review the chart on page 116 and make sure that you use good nonverbal communication as you present.

2. Take turns giving your presentations. As you listen to the presenters, complete a feedback chart like the ones on page 117. Share your assessments with the people in your group.

Self-Assessment		
Yes	**No**	
☐	☐	I successfully identified the meaning of difficult vocabulary from context.
☐	☐	I successfully prepared and gave a presentation.
☐	☐	I was able to use good nonverbal communication during my presentation.
☐	☐	I can use contrastive and emphatic stress.
☐	☐	I can correctly use the target vocabulary words from the unit.

Discussion Questions

With a partner or in a small group, discuss the following questions.

1. Do you think artificial retinas can help people who were born blind?

2. The man in the video could only make out shadows, but the scientist and doctors were excited. Do you think this is a significant advancement in technology?

3. What advances in technology would you like to see next?

The Academic Word List

Words targeted in Level 2 are bold

Word	Sublist	Location
abandon	8	**L2, U4**
abstract	6	L3, U3
academy	5	**L2, U10**
access	4	L0, U5
accommodate	9	L3, U6
accompany	8	L4, U2
accumulate	8	L3, U4
accurate	6	L0, U2
achieve	2	L0, U4
acknowledge	6	L0, U7
acquire	2	L3, U9
adapt	7	L3, U7
adequate	4	L3, U9
adjacent	10	L4, U4
adjust	5	L4, U4
administrate	2	L4, U8
adult	7	L0, U10
advocate	7	L4, U3
affect	2	L1, U1
aggregate	6	L4, U6
aid	7	L0, U5
albeit	10	L4, U3
allocate	6	L3, U6
alter	5	**L2, U6**
alternative	3	L1, U1
ambiguous	8	L4, U7
amend	5	L4, U7
analogy	9	L4, U1
analyze	1	L1, U3
annual	4	L1, U9
anticipate	9	**L2, U8**
apparent	4	**L2, U4**
append	8	L4, U10
appreciate	8	L0, U9
approach	1	L1, U1
appropriate	2	L3, U5
approximate	4	**L2, U7**
arbitrary	8	L4, U7
area	1	L3, U7
aspect	2	**L2, U7**
assemble	10	L3, U1
assess	1	**L2, U8**
assign	6	L3, U5
assist	2	L0, U2
assume	1	L3, U1
assure	9	L4, U8
attach	6	L0, U10

Word	Sublist	Location
attain	9	L3, U5
attitude	4	**L2, U4**
attribute	4	L3, U8
author	6	L0, U1
authority	1	**L2, U2**
automate	8	**L2, U1**
available	1	L0, U8
aware	5	L1, U1
behalf	9	L4, U9
benefit	1	L1, U2
bias	8	L4, U3
bond	6	L4, U9
brief	6	**L2, U9**
bulk	9	L3, U1
capable	6	L3, U5
capacity	5	L3, U2
category	2	**L2, U4**
cease	9	**L2, U2**
challenge	5	L1, U6
channel	7	L4, U5
chapter	2	L0, U2
chart	8	L0, U2
chemical	7	**L2, U6**
circumstance	3	L4, U2
cite	6	L4, U4
civil	4	L3, U2
clarify	8	L3, U7
classic	7	L3, U6
clause	5	L4, U8
code	4	L0, U5
coherent	9	L4, U7
coincide	9	L4, U10
collapse	10	L3, U9
colleague	10	L1, U5
commence	9	**L2, U4**
comment	3	L1, U4
commission	2	L3, U2
commit	4	**L2, U1**
commodity	8	L4, U4
communicate	4	L1, U3
community	2	L1, U4
compatible	9	**L2, U4**
compensate	3	L4, U8
compile	10	L4, U9
complement	8	L4, U8

🔑 Oxford 3000™ words

Word	Sublist	Location
complex	**2**	**L2, U1**
component	3	L3, U1
compound	5	L3, U10
comprehensive	**7**	**L2, U6**
comprise	7	L3, U7
compute	2	L1, U8
conceive	10	L4, U7
concentrate	4	L1, U5
concept	1	L3, U10
conclude	2	L0, U6
concurrent	9	L4, U10
conduct	2	L1, U4
confer	4	L4, U8
confine	9	L4, U8
confirm	7	L1, U8
conflict	5	L1, U7
conform	8	L3, U6
consent	3	L3, U3
consequent	2	L4, U2
considerable	3	L4, U1
consist	1	L1, U9
constant	3	L1, U8
constitute	1	L4, U5
constrain	3	L4, U6
construct	2	L3, U1
consult	**5**	**L2, U8**
consume	**2**	**L2, U6**
contact	5	L1, U4
contemporary	8	L4, U6
context	**1**	**L2, U4**
contract	1	L3, U4
contradict	**8**	**L2, U4**
contrary	7	L3, U1
contrast	4	L3, U2
contribute	3	L1, U9
controversy	**9**	**L2, U9**
convene	3	L4, U1
converse	**9**	**L2, U2**
convert	7	L3, U3
convince	10	L1, U5
cooperate	6	L3, U6
coordinate	**3**	**L2, U2**
core	3	L4, U10
corporate	3	L1, U7
correspond	**3**	**L2, U10**
couple	7	L0, U4
create	1	L3, U7
credit	**2**	**L2, U7**
criteria	3	L3, U2
crucial	8	L3, U7
culture	2	L0, U10

Word	Sublist	Location
currency	8	L2, U3
cycle	4	L3, U5
data	1	L0, U4
debate	4	L3, U5
decade	7	L1, U9
decline	5	L1, U9
deduce	3	L4, U10
define	1	L0, U8
definite	7	L4, U8
demonstrate	3	L1, U2
denote	8	L4, U10
deny	7	L1, U8
depress	10	L0, U8
derive	1	L4, U8
design	2	L0, U10
despite	4	L3, U6
detect	**8**	**L2, U3**
deviate	8	L4, U10
device	9	L0, U2
devote	**9**	**L2, U3**
differentiate	7	L3, U6
dimension	4	L4, U9
diminish	**9**	**L2, U8**
discrete	5	L4, U2
discriminate	6	L4, U5
displace	8	L3, U10
display	6	L0, U8
dispose	7	L4, U1
distinct	2	L4, U2
distort	9	L4, U5
distribute	1	L1, U9
diverse	6	L3, U2
document	3	L0, U4
domain	6	L4, U6
domestic	**4**	**L2, U5**
dominate	3	L3, U7
draft	5	L0, U10
drama	**8**	**L2, U9**
duration	**9**	**L2, U3**
dynamic	7	L3, U3
economy	**1**	**L2, U8**
edit	6	L1, U7
element	2	L3, U1
eliminate	7	L1, U6
emerge	4	L3, U5
emphasis	3	L1, U5
empirical	7	L4, U4
enable	**5**	**L2, U1**
encounter	10	L1, U8

Oxford 3000™ words

Word	Sublist	Location
energy	5	L0, U9
enforce	5	L4, U1
enhance	6	L3, U2
enormous	10	L0, U7
ensure	3	L4, U1
entity	5	L4, U8
environment	1	L1, U1
equate	2	L3, U10
equip	**7**	**L2, U1**
equivalent	5	L1, U7
erode	9	L4, U2
error	4	L0, U2
establish	**1**	**L2, U5**
estate	6	L4, U8
estimate	**1**	**L2, U5**
ethic	9	L3, U4
ethnic	4	L3, U9
evaluate	2	L1, U8
eventual	8	L3, U2
evident	**1**	**L2, U8**
evolve	**5**	**L2, U2**
exceed	6	L1, U10
exclude	3	L3, U8
exhibit	**8**	**L2, U3**
expand	5	L0, U5
expert	6	L0, U3
explicit	6	L4, U3
exploit	8	L4, U9
export	1	L4, U6
expose	5	L4, U1
external	**5**	**L2, U1**
extract	7	L3, U1
facilitate	5	L3, U6
factor	1	L3, U1
feature	2	L0, U2
federal	6	L4, U4
fee	6	L0, U5
file	7	L0, U5
final	2	L0, U1
finance	1	L3, U6
finite	7	L4, U9
flexible	6	L1, U10
fluctuate	8	L4, U10
focus	2	L0, U6
format	**9**	**L2, U8**
formula	1	L3, U5
forthcoming	10	L4, U10
found	9	L0, U7
foundation	7	L1, U9
framework	3	L4, U6

Word	Sublist	Location
function	1	L3, U3
fund	**3**	**L2, U5**
fundamental	5	L1, U8
furthermore	6	L3, U4
gender	6	L3, U8
generate	5	L1, U5
generation	**5**	**L2, U10**
globe	**7**	**L2, U5**
goal	4	L0, U7
grade	7	L0, U3
grant	4	L3, U9
guarantee	7	L1, U7
guideline	8	L1, U6
hence	4	L3, U6
hierarchy	7	L4, U6
highlight	8	L0, U7
hypothesis	4	L3, U4
identical	7	L3, U3
identify	1	L1, U3
ideology	7	L4, U3
ignorance	**6**	**L2, U9**
illustrate	3	L0, U1
image	5	L1, U3
immigrate	3	L4, U7
impact	**2**	**L2, U9**
implement	4	L4, U2
implicate	4	L4, U3
implicit	8	L4, U3
imply	3	L3, U8
impose	4	L3, U10
incentive	6	L4, U2
incidence	6	L3, U4
incline	10	L4, U4
income	1	L0, U4
incorporate	6	L4, U9
index	6	L4, U9
indicate	**1**	**L2, U10**
individual	1	L0, U1
induce	8	L4, U1
inevitable	8	L3, U2
infer	7	L4, U3
infrastructure	8	L4, U1
inherent	9	L4, U7
inhibit	6	L4, U2
initial	3	L0, U3
initiate	6	L3, U8
injure	2	L4, U9
innovate	7	L3, U1

Word	Sublist	Location		Word	Sublist	Location
input	6	L2, U5		maximize	3	L1, U9
insert	7	L2, U7		mechanism	4	L3, U3
insight	9	L3, U4		🔑 media	7	L0, U8
inspect	8	L4, U9		mediate	9	L4, U10
🔑 instance	3	L3, U3		🔑 medical	5	L1, U2
🔑 institute	2	L1, U6		🔑 medium	9	L1, U10
instruct	6	L1, U6		🔑 **mental**	5	**L2, U6**
integral	9	L4, U6		🔑 method	1	L1, U2
integrate	4	L4, U6		migrate	6	L4, U1
integrity	10	**L2, U1**		🔑 **military**	9	**L2, U3**
🔑 intelligence	6	L0, U10		minimal	9	L1, U9
🔑 intense	8	L3, U7		minimize	8	L3, U1
interact	3	**L2, U3**		🔑 minimum	6	L1, U10
intermediate	9	**L2, U5**		🔑 ministry	6	L4, U6
🔑 internal	4	L1, U10		🔑 minor	3	L0, U7
interpret	1	L3, U10		mode	7	L4, U5
🔑 interval	6	L3, U10		modify	5	L1, U6
intervene	7	L3, U6		🔑 monitor	5	L3, U4
intrinsic	10	L4, U7		**motive**	6	**L2, U7**
🔑 invest	2	L3, U2		**mutual**	9	**L2, U2**
🔑 **investigate**	4	**L2, U9**				
invoke	10	L4, U5		negate	3	L4, U4
🔑 involve	1	L3, U7		🔑 **network**	5	**L2, U2**
isolate	7	L3, U2		**neutral**	6	**L2, U5**
🔑 issue	1	L0, U3		🔑 nevertheless	6	L3, U5
🔑 item	2	L0, U6		nonetheless	10	L4, U5
				norm	9	L4, U7
🔑 job	4	L0, U10		🔑 normal	2	L0, U6
journal	2	L1, U10		🔑 notion	5	L3, U5
🔑 justify	3	L4, U2		notwithstanding	10	L4, U6
				🔑 nuclear	8	L3, U9
🔑 label	4	L0, U1				
🔑 **labor**	1	**L2, U4**		🔑 objective	5	L0, U4
🔑 layer	3	L3, U3		🔑 obtain	2	L3, U4
🔑 lecture	6	L0, U6		🔑 obvious	4	L1, U7
🔑 legal	1	L1, U2		🔑 occupy	4	L4, U8
legislate	1	L4, U1		🔑 **occur**	1	**L2, U10**
levy	10	L4, U3		🔑 odd	10	L1, U8
🔑 liberal	5	L4, U3		offset	8	L4, U9
🔑 license	5	L3, U8		**ongoing**	10	**L2, U7**
likewise	10	L3, U4		🔑 option	4	L1, U10
🔑 link	3	L0, U4		orient	5	L4, U4
🔑 locate	3	L1, U4		**outcome**	3	**L2, U7**
🔑 logic	5	L3, U5		🔑 **output**	4	**L2, U5**
				🔑 **overall**	4	**L2, U9**
🔑 maintain	2	L1, U10		**overlap**	9	**L2, U4**
🔑 major	1	L3, U7		🔑 **overseas**	6	**L2, U3**
manipulate	8	L4, U10				
manual	9	L2, U10		🔑 panel	10	L4, U5
margin	5	**L2, U3**		paradigm	7	L4, U2
mature	9	**L2, U8**		paragraph	8	L1, U7

🔑 Oxford 3000™ words